Department of Energy
FY 2014 Congressional Budget Request

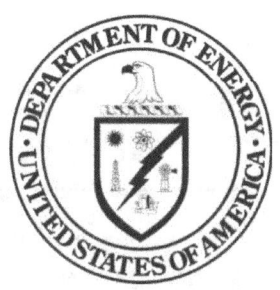

Budget Highlights

April 2013   Office of Chief Financial Officer

Table of Contents

INTRODUCTION 1

DEPARTMENT OF ENERGY BUDGET BY ORGANIZATION 13

DEPARTMENT OF ENERGY BUDGET BY APPROPRIATION 14

NATIONAL NUCLEAR SECURITY ADMINISTRATION 16

    WEAPONS ACTIVITIES 17

    DEFENSE NUCLEAR NONPROLIFERATION 20

    NAVAL REACTORS 24

    OFFICE OF THE ADMINISTRATOR – NNSA 26

ENERGY EFFICIENCY AND RENEWABLE ENERGY 27

ELECTRICITY DELIVERY AND ENERGY RELIABILITY 31

FOSSIL ENERGY 33

NUCLEAR ENERGY 36

RACE TO THE TOP FOR ENERGY EFFICIENCY AND GRID MODERNIZATION 38

ENVIRONMENTAL MANAGEMENT 39

LEGACY MANAGEMENT 42

ADVANCED RESEARCH PROJECTS AGENCY – ENERGY 43

SCIENCE 44

DEPARTMENTAL ADMINISTRATION 46

HEARINGS AND APPEALS 47

ADVANCED TECHNOLOGY VEHICLES MANUFACTURING LOAN PROGRAM 48

INNOVATIVE TECHNOLOGY LOAN GUARANTEE PROGRAM 49

HEALTH, SAFETY AND SECURITY 50

ENERGY INFORMATION ADMINISTRATION 52

INSPECTOR GENERAL 53

POWER MARKETING ADMINISTRATIONS 54

FEDERAL ENERGY REGULATORY COMMISSION 56

INVESTING FOR SECURITY AND PROSPERITY

The United States is in a global competition to capture the energy jobs of the 21st century. In March, 2013, President Obama updated his "Blueprint for a Secure Energy Future" and laid out an investment strategy for his "all-of-the-above" approach to develop every source of American energy in a safe and responsible way – investing in new clean energy technologies and expanding oil and gas production. It is a winning strategy for the economy, energy security, and the environment. The President's goals include:

- Reducing our overall dependence on oil by more than 2 million barrels a day by 2025, and reducing oil imports by half by 2020
- Doubling renewable electricity production from wind, solar and geothermal by 2020
- Doubling energy productivity by 2030

The Department of Energy (DOE) brings some of the nation's best scientific minds and capabilities to bear to address our energy challenges and implement the President's strategy for growing our economy and ensuring our national security. DOE's mission is to advance the energy, environmental, and nuclear security of the United States; promote scientific and technological innovation in support of that mission; and ensure the environmental cleanup of the national nuclear weapons complex. It facilitates many of the President's highest priorities, including cutting carbon pollution, increasing climate preparedness, supporting clean energy and innovation, and protecting Americans from the threat of nuclear harm and pollution, which are critical to job creation, long-term economic growth, and national security.

In total, the President's 2014 Budget provides $28.4 billion in discretionary funds for DOE to support its mission. This amount includes $11.7 billion for nuclear security. The FY 2014 Request supports the President's goal to increase American competitiveness and reduce our reliance on oil by making strategic investments in critical research and technology sectors for clean energy and to make significant national security advances to leave future generations with a country that is safer, healthier, and more prosperous. Further, the President proposes investments so the United States will lead the world in research, development, demonstration, and deployment of

The Fiscal Year 2014 Budget Request

The President's 2014 Budget for the Department of Energy advances the energy, environmental, and nuclear security of the United States; promotes scientific and technical innovation in support of that mission; and ensures environmental cleanup of the nuclear weapons complex. It continues to facilitate many of the President's highest priorities, including cutting carbon pollution, increasing climate preparedness, supporting clean energy and innovation, and reducing the threat of nuclear weapons, which are critical to job creation, long-term economic growth, and national security.

✓ Invests in Clean Energy, Innovation, and Jobs of the Future

✓ Cuts Wasteful Spending and Improves Efficiency

✓ Protects Americans from the Threat of Nuclear Harm and Pollution

✓ Makes Progress toward the Long Term Disposal of Nuclear Waste

clean energy technologies, supporting a reduction in dependence on oil and mitigating the impact of climate change. In light of the current discretionary spending caps, these increases in funding are significant and a testament to the importance of clean energy and innovation to the country's economic future and the importance of nuclear security to the Nation's safety.

The Administration's comprehensive strategy for clean energy starts with basic and applied research to address some of the fundamental unknowns to advancing clean energy technologies, such as how to develop advanced light-weight, ultra-strong materials. The strategy also includes research and development to create improved clean energy products, such as solar panels, batteries and electric vehicles, wind turbines, and advanced small modular nuclear reactors.   In addition, the Administration's clean energy strategy provides appropriate assistance to American entrepreneurs to commercialize and manufacture the technologies that will lead the world in a new, clean energy economy.

Innovation is similarly fundamental to the national security missions of the Department. The National Nuclear Security Administration (NNSA) harnesses science and technology to reduce nuclear dangers and to maintain a safe, secure, and effective nuclear stockpile, without the use of underground nuclear testing. NNSA supports the President's pledge to lead an international effort to secure vulnerable nuclear materials by December 2013. This Budget Request would fulfill the President's commitment.

Investing in Clean Energy, Innovation, and Jobs of the Future

"After years of talking about it, we're finally poised to take control of our energy future. We produce more oil than we have in 15 years. We import less oil than we have in 20 years. We've doubled the amount of renewable energy that we generate from sources like wind and solar -- with tens of thousands of good jobs to show for it. We're producing more natural gas than we ever have before -- with hundreds of thousands of good jobs to show for it. We supported the first new nuclear power plant in America since the 1970s. And we're sending less carbon pollution into the environment than we have in nearly 20 years."
– President Obama, March 15, Argonne National Laboratory

The United States is on the path to a cleaner and more secure energy future. But even with this progress, there is more work to do. Rising gas prices serve as a reminder that we are still too reliant on oil, which comes at a cost to American families and businesses. While there is no overnight solution to address rising gas prices in the short term, President Obama has reiterated his commitment to a sustained, all-of-the-above energy strategy and urged Congress to take up common-sense proposals that will further reduce our dependence on oil, better protect consumers from spikes in gas prices, and reduce pollution.

The missions of DOE's applied energy programs are to deliver research, development and demonstration of efficiency and renewable energy, advanced fossil, nuclear, and grid technologies. Partnered with world class innovators, entrepreneurs, engineers, scientists, and workers and applying multidisciplinary approaches, these programs provide the needed focus to address our Nation's energy security and environmental goals. The FY 2014 Budget for these applied programs includes $4.7 billion, a 42 percent increase over FY 2012 current levels, for investments needed to advance energy security.

Office of Energy Efficiency and Renewable Energy: Funding Clean Energy Research, Development, and Demonstration to Keep America Competitive and Respond to the Threat of Climate Change
The Office of Energy Efficiency and Renewable Energy (EERE) is the U.S. government's primary clean energy technology organization responsible for supporting high-impact applied Research, Development, Demonstration and Deployment (RDD&D) in the areas of sustainable transportation, renewable electricity, and end-use energy efficiency in buildings and factories. Partnered with world class innovators, entrepreneurs, engineers, scientists and workers, all applying multidisciplinary approaches, EERE provides the needed focus to address our Nation's energy security, environmental, and economic goals:

- Providing American businesses and households with cleaner and low-cost energy alternatives by creating both low cost renewable supplies and energy efficient products and systems;
- Reducing impacts on the U.S. economy from price and supply uncertainties associated with the global petroleum market;
- Ensuring diversity and choice in the way energy services are produced; and
- Developing approaches that accelerate economic growth and job creation while improving the environment by reducing greenhouse gas emissions and improving air and water quality.

EERE is positioned to help achieve these goals through this Budget by developing and accelerating the adoption of a new generation of energy technologies — technologies that will make our buildings, factories, power plants, and vehicles cleaner and more efficient and productive. EERE's work helps ensure that U.S. manufacturers and U.S. workers lead in the global energy race for and secure the benefits of a clean, domestically powered energy system as a foundation for a clean and secure American future. The challenges and opportunities faced today by the U.S. demand continued targeted Federal investments in high-impact clean energy technologies and approaches where manufacturing/technology leadership will likely be won or lost within the next 5 to 10 years, in addition to setting the stage for American energy technology leadership in the decades to come.

The FY 2014 Budget Request of $2.8 billion for EERE is aimed at accelerating innovative change within the Nation's energy economy. The Request includes funding for programs associated with meeting the President's goals of investing in the next generation of renewable energy technologies, advanced vehicles and fuels, and energy efficiency measures that reduce energy use in Federal agencies and the industrial and building sectors. Within EERE, the Budget increases funding by 75 percent above 2012 levels for development and demonstration of the next generation of advanced vehicles and by 42 percent for the next generation of advanced biofuels and biorefineries. It increases funding by 29 percent for innovative projects to make clean, renewable power, such as solar energy and off-shore wind, more easily integrated into the electric grid and as affordable as electricity from conventional sources, without subsidies. It doubles funding for energy efficiency and advanced manufacturing activities to help reduce energy use and costs in commercial and residential buildings, in the industrial and business sectors, and in Federal buildings and fleets. These investments will support progress toward the President's goal of cutting in half the energy wasted by our homes and businesses, doubling our energy productivity over the next 20 years.

Working to Enhance American Manufacturing

EERE is committed to manufacturing competitiveness efforts across all of its programs to help the U.S. compete in the growing global market for clean energy products and technologies, and to significantly enhance the energy competitiveness and productivity of the U.S. manufacturing sector. In this Budget, EERE seeks to build on past successes, including:

Innovative Manufacturing Initiative. In 2012 EERE invested $54 million on 13 projects to spur development of transformational manufacturing technologies. These innovations address core technical issues facing U.S. manufacturers—enabling significant gains in energy productivity, environmental performance, product yield, and economic growth. This investment will help to provide American manufacturers with the cutting-edge tools, techniques and processes they need to compete successfully in the global marketplace.

Building a Wind Energy Sector. In 2005 EERE invested in fabrication processes for significantly longer wind turbine blades and from 2008 to 2012 it supported blade manufacturing R&D including advanced modular automation, advanced mold operations, and non-destructive inspection. Based on strong innovation supporting policies, and key tax incentives, wind power manufacturing has been growing in the United States. Between 2005 and 2011, the U.S. wind market grew from approximately $2 billion to $9 billion, while the value of wind equipment installed in U.S. wind farms that was manufactured in the U.S. doubled from roughly 35 percent to 70 percent.

Creating a Strong Solar Industry through Public Private Partnerships. In 2011 EERE began a five-year, $110 million investment in the SunShot Photovoltaic Manufacturing Initiative which established manufacturing development facilities and industry consortia to provide infrastructure for demonstrating, testing, and optimizing new PV manufacturing technologies with reduced capital requirements. In 2011 EERE also invested $20.3 million in High Impact PV Supply Chain R&D aimed at strengthening U.S. photovoltaic manufacturing by supporting improved yield and high-volume production.

In FY 2014, EERE investment decisions will continue to be based on DOE and independent economic analysis and assessments for potential technology impacts on energy usage, market penetration, manufacturing competitiveness and chance of success. This approach is focused on the most promising opportunities across a full spectrum of sectors and maturation timeframes to ensure both a full pipeline of more efficient technologies and market adoption of renewables. The portfolio maintains critical activities in focused technology areas identified by past Budget Requests, including off-shore wind, drop-in biofuels, and solar energy and manufacturing.

In addition to supporting aggressive RDD&D in each of EERE's technology specific offices, this Budget Request reflects increased focus on high-impact new cross-cutting efforts that are breaking down the silos between EERE's technology specific offices. These cross-cutting initiatives include:

- **EV Everywhere Grand Challenge** — a DOE-wide cross-cutting initiative focused on breakthroughs in plug-in electric vehicle technology to achieve the goal of making the U.S. the first country in the world to invent and produce plug-in electric vehicles that are as affordable and convenient as gasoline powered vehicles by 2022.
- **Clean Energy Manufacturing Initiative** – a new cross-cutting EERE initiative focused on dramatically improving U.S. competitiveness in the manufacturing of clean energy products (like solar modules, LED's, batteries, and wind blades) and strengthening U.S. competitiveness across multiple manufacturing industries through increased energy productivity. This initiative is a strategic integration of efforts in EERE's Advanced Manufacturing Office and technology specific offices.
- **EERE Grid Integration Initiative** — a cross-cutting and integrated initiative in vehicles, solar, and buildings addressing grid integration barriers and opportunities associated with variable, distributed renewable energy generators, electric vehicle charging, and building efficiency and controls. These activities seek to develop technologies, tools, and approaches that overcome grid integration barriers associated with EERE technologies, that key stakeholders achieve the confidence within their risk tolerance necessary to install high penetrations of clean energy technologies while maintaining grid reliability.
- **Wide Bandgap Semiconductors for Clean Energy Initiative** — Wide bandgap semiconductor technology, which was initially developed for military and solid-state lighting uses, is a key next-generation platform for semiconductors devices that offers the potential for high-power-conversion electronics that are much more compact and efficient and can operate at much higher temperatures and voltages. This revolutionary technology has the potential to be a platform the next generation of electric drivetrains, solar inverters, high efficiency motors, solid-state transformers for the grid, and many other critical clean energy applications.

Investing in energy efficiency and renewable energy generation are fundamental steps necessary for creating a clean energy economy. In other parts of the Budget, the Administration continues to call on Congress to pass HomeStar or similar mandatory funding legislation aimed at creating jobs and spurring economic growth by encouraging Americans to invest in energy-saving home improvements. The Budget also invests $2 billion over the next ten years from Federal oil and gas development revenue in a new Energy Security Trust that would provide a reliable stream of mandatory funding for R&D on cost-effective transportation alternatives that reduce our dependence on oil. It would be designed to invest in research that will improve and reduce the cost of the technologies of the future—technologies that will allow us to run our cars and trucks on electricity, homegrown biofuels, fuel cells, and domestically produced natural gas. In addition, the Administration proposes to repeal a number of inefficient tax preferences available for fossil fuels production and to help transition to a clean energy economy.

Advanced Research Projects Agency – Energy: Changing What's Possible
The FY 2014 Budget Request includes $379 million for the Advanced Research Projects Agency – Energy (ARPA-E). ARPA-E supports high-impact energy research with real-world applications in areas including power electronics, batteries for electrical energy storage, battery management and sensing, grid networking technology, thermal energy storage, carbon capture technologies, natural gas vehicles, non-photosynthetic biofuels, and rare earth alternatives. ARPA-E is funding transformational research to create revolutionary technologies that will fuel the economy, create new jobs, reduce energy imports, improve energy efficiency, reduce energy-related emissions, and ensure that the U.S. maintains a technological lead in developing and deploying advanced energy technologies. ARPA-E projects have demonstrated major technical successes and garnered private sector interest within only four years of the agency's creation. Some of the significant ARPA-E technical achievements include:

- Doubling the world record energy density for a rechargeable lithium-ion battery (to 400 Whr/kg);
- Developing a 1 megawatt silicon carbide transistor the size of a fingernail;
- Engineering microbes that use hydrogen and carbon dioxide to make liquid transportation fuel, and;
- Pioneering a near-isothermal compressed air energy storage system.

ARPA-E performers have also made important commercial progress. Reflecting the progress these projects have made toward developing new technologies that could transform the way Americans use and produce energy, 12 awardees have leveraged their ARPA-E supported technologies to form new companies, 10 awardees have partnered with other government agencies for later stage investment; and 17 new technologies have attracted over $450 million in private sector follow-on funding after ARPA-E's initial investment of approximately $70 million.

Race to the Top for Energy Efficiency and Grid Modernization
Challenging States to Cut Energy Waste and Support Energy Efficiency and Modernizing the Grid

Vision: Double energy productivity from the 2010 level by 2030.

Challenge: To accelerate increases in energy productivity at the state, local, or tribal level through policy actions that can address market barriers to investment in energy efficiency, clean energy deployment, and grid modernization.

Objective: Motivate states, tribes, local governments with public power authority, and co-operatives to align the incentives of their organizations, regulated utilities, and other investors with (1) the interests of customers/members in energy efficiency and distributed generation, and (2) the national interest in clean energy and a more resilient and efficient grid.

Opportunity: DOE can engage state governors as well as electric co-operatives, public power authorities, and tribes through a challenge similar to the Department of Education's Race to the Top, offering informational resources and merit-based technical assistance grants to support interested applicants to help them qualify to compete for awards by adopting targeted policies. These awards will be made to the applicants that make the most progress toward improving energy productivity.

Qualifying criteria: The challenge to states and other applicants will be presented as qualifying criteria in five categories: energy efficiency, including combined heat and power, and demand response; distributed generation; customer access to data; resiliency and cybersecurity; and visibility in grid operations. Applicants will have access to relevant DOE informational resources and will be eligible to receive technical assistance grants based on the merits of their initial plan for policy and regulatory changes.

Selection criteria: Applicants that make the most progress toward improving energy productivity will be rewarded with federal funds. Regional diversity may be a factor in selection, and regional variations in weather and the composition of economic activity will be taken into consideration.

Awards: $200 million will be split between (a) merit-based technical assistance grants in the qualifying phase, and (b) awards based on demonstrated performance in the final selection. Because applicants vary widely in size, awards may be proportional to each successful applicant's size.

Office of Electricity Delivery and Energy Reliability: Enabling a Clean Energy Economy

The Office of Electricity Delivery and Energy Reliability (OE) is responsible for leading national efforts to modernize the electricity grid, enhance the security of energy infrastructure, and facilitate recovery from disruptions to the energy supply. The Department's FY 2014 Budget Request for OE of $169 million, a 24 percent increase over the FY 2012 level, ensures that progress continues toward one of the Nation's key enablers of a clean energy economy – the electricity delivery system.

The U.S. electricity grid, built with technology designed for the demands of an earlier era, is facing many new and complex challenges. To increase efficiency and enable greater use of renewable and other energy sources while maintaining the reliability, security, and affordability of electric power delivery, OE develops 'next generation' technologies and management approaches, works with stakeholders to facilitate development of reliable electricity infrastructure, and strengthens the physical and cyber security of the Nation's energy delivery system. The FY 2014 Budget would fund new efforts to produce real-time analysis of the transmission system and energy supply disruptions, improve response times during emergencies, and promote effective cybersecurity capabilities in the energy sector.

Office of Fossil Energy: Supporting Critical Carbon Capture Research Initiatives and Ensuring American Energy Options

The FY 2014 Budget Request of $638 million for the Office of Fossil Energy (FE) is to advance technologies related to the reliable, efficient, affordable, and environmentally sound use of fossil fuels as well as manage the Strategic Petroleum Reserve and Northeast Home Heating oil Reserve to provide strategic and economic security against disruptions in U.S. oil supplies. The Budget provides $421 million for the Fossil Energy Research and Development program including an investment of $266 million in research and development primarily dedicated to developing cost-effective carbon capture and storage and advanced power systems. The Budget includes a one-time, $25 million inducement prize for the first natural gas combined cycle power plant to integrate large-scale carbon capture and storage. The Budget also includes $12 million to fund DOE's participation in a multi-agency research initiative aimed at advancing technology and methods to safely and responsibly develop America's natural gas resources. Specifically, DOE, in collaboration with the Environmental Protection Agency and the Department of Interior, will focus on minimizing the health, safety, and environmental effects of natural gas and oil production from hydraulic fracturing

Supporting American Energy
In FY 2012, the office of Fossil Energy achieved the following:
✓ Conducted over 2,000 hours of post-combustion capture pilot-scale testing;
✓ Initiated large-scale projects to inject, monitor, and store carbon dioxide at two additional Regional Carbon Sequestration Partnerships (RCSP);
✓ Completed a 30-day natural gas production test of an arctic well, providing large volumes of data available to the public for further evaluation;
✓ Completed replacement storage cavern at Bayou Choctaw Strategic Petroleum Reserve site to maintain emergency response readiness of oil reserves; and
✓ Loaned 121,000 barrels of Northeast Home Heating Oil Reserve's inventory to DoD in support of FEMA's response to Hurricane Sandy aftermath.

in shale and other geologic formations. In addition, $197 million will provide for national and regional energy security through the continued operations of the Strategic Petroleum Reserve and Northeast Home Heating Oil Reserve.

Office of Nuclear Energy: Investing in Energy Innovation and Technical Leadership

Currently, nuclear energy supplies approximately 20 percent of the Nation's electricity and over 70 percent of clean, non-carbon producing electricity. Over 100 nuclear power plants are offering reliable and affordable baseload electricity in the United States, and they are doing so without air pollution and greenhouse gas emissions. The Office of Nuclear Energy (NE) supports research, development, and demonstration activities which are designed to resolve the technical, cost, safety, waste management, proliferation resistance, and security challenges of continued use of nuclear energy. NE leads the Federal research effort to develop nuclear energy technologies, including generation, safety, waste storage and management, and security technologies. These efforts s are intended to ensure a clean, safe, secure, and affordable nuclear energy capability.

The Department requests $735 million in FY 2014 for the Office of Nuclear Energy (NE), including $24 million from the Nuclear Waste Fund. As in FY 2013, the Department is requesting funding for Idaho National Laboratory Site Wide Safeguards and Security ($94M) within the NE appropriation. A prerequisite to the continued use of nuclear power is public confidence in the safety of nuclear plants and commercial confidence that the plants can be operated safely, reliably and economically. The Department will explore improvements to light water reactor systems and fuel forms to further enhance safety and reliability under severe accident conditions. R&D efforts will be coordinated with reactor vendors, utilities, universities, regulators and the international community to ensure that lessons learned from the events at Fukushima, Japan are appropriately incorporated and that these efforts are integrated and efficient. The Request also includes $70 million to continue support for design certification and licensing activities for Small Modular Reactor designs through cost-shared arrangements with industry partners. The Request also funds activities to lay the ground work for the design of an integrated waste management system, and related research and development activities, as discussed in further detail on page 12.

Loan Programs Office: Managing Clean Energy Investments and Financing Vehicles Technologies

In FY 2014, DOE continues its focus on effectively deploying its remaining $170 million in credit subsidy and $34 billion in loan authority in the nuclear power, front-end nuclear, fossil, and renewable and energy efficiency sectors. The FY 2014 Budget Requests $48 million to support both continuing origination activities and a fully staffed portfolio management function. The Request is expected to be offset by collections from borrowers authorized under the Title XVII of the Energy Policy Act of 2005 (P.L. 109-8). In addition, the Department Requests $6 million to support ongoing due diligence and monitoring activities associated with making loans to automobile and automobile part manufacturers to produce advanced technology vehicles or qualified components.

Investing in Science and Innovation to Keep America Competitive

"The world is shifting to an innovation economy, and nobody does innovation better than America. In today's innovation economy, we also need a world-class commitment to science and research." – President Obama, Osawatomie, KS, December 6, 2011

Office of Science: Delivering Scientific Discovery and User Facilities to Advance American Competitiveness

With a history of supporting research leading to over 100 Nobel Prizes—20 in the past 10 years, the Department's Office of Science is the largest federal sponsor of basic research in the physical sciences, providing about 45 percent of such funding to some 25,000 researchers at 17 DOE National Laboratories and more than 300 universities nationwide. The Office oversees 10 of the Department's National Laboratories and constructs and operates the world's most formidable array of major scientific user facilities—including large particle accelerators, advanced x-ray light sources, several of the world's fastest supercomputers, reactors and neutron scattering sources, and sophisticated facilities for nanoscience and genomics—used by 29,000 researchers across the Nation. The Department's Office of Science forms a crucial mainstay of U.S. leadership in science—and a foundation of American innovation and prosperity. The Office is also the lead federal agency supporting fundamental, transformative research in the vital field of energy.

The FY 2014 Budget provides $5.2 billion to sustain and advance this investment in America's prosperity, economic competitiveness, and energy future. Today, nations across the world are increasing their investments in R&D. At the same time, we stand on the threshold of a revolution in energy technologies.

The development of truly transformative new energy technologies will require breakthroughs in basic science. The promise for energy innovation—and indeed for technological innovation across many sectors of the American economy—lies with today's powerful new scientific capabilities to observe, characterize, and manipulate matter at the atomic and molecular scales. These new capabilities provide researchers with an unprecedented ability to lay the scientific foundation for the development of revolutionary new materials, new products, and improved energy sources and processes. Combined with the power of today's supercomputer modeling and simulation, these new capabilities are enabling us to accelerate

---

DOE Light Sources Cultivate a Quartet of Nobel Prizes

Millions of times brighter than medical x-rays, five DOE synchrotron light sources generate high-quality, stable beams of x-rays that have become our principal means of unraveling the identities and positions of atoms in crystallized samples ranging from relatively simple metals to highly complex biological molecules like proteins and DNA.

Today, DOE light sources are world leaders in macromolecular crystallography because the high brightness x-ray sources enable rapid screening of crystals and the collection of high quality data sets from even very small crystals. The explosion of information from DOE light sources has enabled researchers to unlock some of nature's most guarded secrets, four of which have been recognized in the past decade by Nobel Prizes in Chemistry.

- 2012, Studies of G-protein–coupled receptors (Lefkowitz and Kobilka).
- 2009, Studies of the structure and function of the ribosome (Ramakrishnan, Steitz, and Yonath).
- 2006, Studies of the molecular basis of eukaryotic transcription (Kornberg).
- 2003, Structural and mechanistic studies of ion channels (MacKinnon).

The five DOE light sources are the Advanced Light Source at Lawrence Berkeley National Laboratory, the Advanced Photon Source at Argonne National Laboratory, the National Synchrotron Light Source at Brookhaven National Laboratory, and the Stanford Synchrotron Radiation Lightsource and Linac Coherent Light Source at SLAC National Accelerator Laboratory.

---

breakthroughs in a wide range of fields. The Office of Science is taking advantage of these new capabilities on multiple fronts. The Budget provides continued support for the Energy Frontier Research Centers. These Centers—involving some 600 researchers from multiple institutions—have proved scientifically productive, generating some 3,400 peer-reviewed publications, 60 invention disclosures, 200 patents, and numerous instances of technology transfer in just three years. The Budget also supports two Energy Innovation Hubs—the Joint Center on Artificial Photosynthesis led by the California Institute of Technology in partnership with Lawrence Berkeley National Laboratory, which is at the cutting edge of the effort to produce fuels directly from sunlight; and the Joint Center for Energy Storage Research, led by Argonne National Laboratory, which has brought together leading researchers in an aggressive push for radically improved batteries for both transportation and the electric grid. Meanwhile, the three DOE BioEnergy Research Centers are producing breakthroughs leading to improvements in plant feedstocks, deconstruction, and fuel synthesis for advanced biofuels, laying the foundation for a new biofuels economy. The Budget also continues to invest in research and facilities to advance our scientific understanding of fusion energy.

Scientific leadership today depends on access to the unique research tools provided by our major scientific user facilities. The Budget will support completion of the National Synchrotron Light Source II at Brookhaven National Laboratory, which will deliver x-ray beams of ultra-high brightness and enable researchers to penetrate more deeply into the secrets of matter. Having deployed the world's fastest and fourth fastest supercomputers, the Titan at Oak Ridge National Laboratory and Mira at Argonne, the Office continues to press forward with efforts to maintain America's lead and take maximum scientific advantage of computing capabilities. The Budget advances several other major facilities construction projects, including an upgrade to the Advanced Photon Source at Argonne, an upgrade to the Continuous Electron Beam Accelerator Facility at Thomas Jefferson National Accelerator Facility, and construction of the ITER international fusion experiment.

Many of the tools and the concepts of today's use-inspired and energy-oriented research are outgrowths of science originally aimed at pure discovery. The Budget provides continued strong support for efforts to expand our fundamental understanding of the universe and matter through research in high energy physics and nuclear physics—which has yielded several headline-making discoveries in just this past year. The Office of Science continues to foster the synergies between these discovery-driven disciplines and the work of more use-inspired researchers—synergies that have been a key to the unique vitality of American science.

DOE Computers Dominate November 2012 Top500 list.

DOE's Oak Ridge National Laboratory (ORNL), Lawrence Livermore National Laboratory (LLNL) and Argonne National Laboratory (ANL) put the Department back on top of the world's most powerful supercomputers as measured by the November 2012 Top500 list, with ORNL's Titan topping the list at 27 petaflops, LLNL's Sequoia second at 20 petaflops and ANL's Mira fourth at 10 petaflops. Sequoia, the LLNL machine, is dedicated to the Department's national security mission while Titan and Mira are open to researchers from universities, private industry, small business, and government laboratories for a wide array of science and engineering inquiry that can only be conducted via high performance computing — from astrophysics to seismology — and including numerous projects focused on energy, carbon sequestration, and advanced manufacturing.

Protecting Americans from the Threat of Nuclear Harm and Pollution

As outlined in the *Nuclear Posture Review* and echoed in the 2012 Department of Defense Strategic Guidance, the United States seeks to maintain a safe, secure and effective nuclear deterrent, while reducing the role and number of nuclear weapons and countering the threat of nuclear proliferation by both regional state actors and terrorists. As a component of this agenda, the Administration is reducing its nuclear force to comply with the limits of the New Strategic Arms Reduction Treaty (New START) with Russia, which reduces the maximum number of strategic nuclear weapons each country can deploy to 1,550.

The Department's National Nuclear Security Administration (NNSA) achieved significant milestones during FY 2012, and is building on those accomplishments in FY 2013, to leverage science to maintain our nation's nuclear deterrence and reduce the risks of proliferation. Additionally, the Environmental Management program made progress advancing responsible nuclear cleanup from the Cold War and has reduced DOE's cleanup footprint by more than 70 percent. The Department's FY 2014 Budget Request seeks to build upon these successes and further advance the President's nuclear security agenda.

National Nuclear Security Administration: Modernizing the Nation's Nuclear Deterrent and Securing Vulnerable Nuclear Materials

The NNSA is critical to ensuring the security and safety of our nation. The NNSA implements programs for three major national security endeavors: leveraging science to maintain a safe, secure and effective arsenal of nuclear weapons and capabilities to deter any adversary and guarantee that defense to our allies; accelerating and expanding our efforts at home and around the world to reduce the global threat posed by nuclear weapons, nuclear proliferation and unsecured or excess nuclear materials; and, providing safe and effective nuclear propulsion for the U.S. Navy.

The FY 2014 President's Budget Request for NNSA is $11.7 billion, an increase of $647 million (6 percent) from FY 2012 current levels. Funds are requested in four accounts:

- Weapons Activities: $7.9 billion, $311 million (4 percent) higher than the FY 2013 annualized CR level of $7.6 billion.
- Defense Nuclear Nonproliferation: $2.1 billion, $161 million (7 percent) lower than the FY 2012 current level of $2.3 billion.
- Naval Reactors: $1.2 billion, $166 million (15 percent) higher than the FY 2012 current level of $1.1 billion
- Office of the Administrator: $398 million, $12 million (3 percent) lower than the FY 2012 current level of $410 million

Modernizing the Nuclear Security Enterprise

The FY 2014 Budget Request advances the Department's commitment to the national security interests of the United States through stewardship of a safe, secure and effective nuclear weapons stockpile as a consequence of the New START Treaty and promotes the goal to reduce the role of nuclear weapons in our national security strategy. As the United States reduces its nuclear stockpile, the science, technology and engineering capabilities and intellectual capacity within the nuclear security enterprise become more critical to sustaining the U.S. nuclear deterrent. NNSA continues to emphasize these capabilities, including functioning as a national science, technology, and engineering resource on nuclear issues to other agencies with national security responsibilities. This Budget reflects an investment strategy that provides a strong basis for maintaining a safe, secure and effective nuclear stockpile without additional nuclear testing; strengthening the science technology and engineering base; modernizing the physical infrastructure; and streamlining the enterprise's physical and operational footprint.

Through the NNSA, the Department requests $7.9 billion for the Weapons Activities appropriation, a 4 percent, or $311 million, increase over the FY 2013 annualized CR level. This

---

Reaffirming Our Commitment to Stockpile Modernization

In his 2013 State of the Union address, the President pledged to "engage Russia to seek further reductions in our nuclear arsenals." To ensure that reductions can be made without adding unacceptable levels of risk to the stockpile, the Administration has pledged to modernize the U.S. nuclear weapons inventory over the next decade. This Request continues to support such ambitious goals.

- As long as nuclear weapons remain in existence, the U.S. will maintain a safe, secure, and effective arsenal. To that end, the Request funds our Stockpile Stewardship and Management Program, including high priority Life Extension Programs (LEPs) for the B61 and W76 warheads, a life extension study for the W78/88-1, and the ALT 370 for the W88.

- NNSA physically dismantles weapons to meet the U.S. obligations under New Start and is on schedule to dismantle by 2022 all weapons retired before 2009.

- The Budget funds critical infrastructure modernization efforts, including the Uranium Capabilities Replacement Project (formerly the Uranium Processing Facility), and commits NNSA to optimizing the use of existing facilities to accomplish its missions and provide the capabilities needed to sustain the Nuclear Security Enterprise now and in the future.

funding proposal is the result of an unprecedented cooperative analysis and planning process jointly conducted by the National Nuclear Security Administration (NNSA) and the Department of Defense (DoD). The Budget meets the *Nuclear Posture Review* (NPR) goals of sustaining the stockpile and modernizing the infrastructure by funding the life extension programs for the W76, B61, and W78 nuclear weapons; improving or replacing aging facilities with such projects as the Uranium Processing Facility; adding funds for tritium production and plutonium manufacturing and experimentation; and funding the stewardship capabilities that sustain the stockpile without new underground nuclear testing. To meet the NPR goals but still stay within the tight discretionary spending caps now in place, the Budget proposes to achieve savings through a strong synergy and alignment among science, engineering, technology development and manufacturing capabilities with life extension programs, and by implementing several management efficiencies and reducing work on lower priority efforts.

The Naval Reactors program ensures the safe and reliable operation of reactor plants in nuclear-powered submarines and aircraft carriers, constituting over 40 percent of the U.S. Navy's combatants, and fulfills the Navy's requirements for new nuclear propulsion plants that meet current and future national defense requirements. The FY 2014 Budget Request for Naval Reactors (NR) is $1.2 billion, an increase of $166 million, or 15 percent, above the 2012 current level. NR is responsible for all naval nuclear propulsion work, beginning with reactor plant technology development and design, continuing through reactor plant operation and maintenance, and ending with reactor plant disposal. NR's Request supports the core objective of ensuring the safe and reliable operation of the Nation's nuclear fleet and includes continued funding for reactor systems development for the replacement of the OHIO-class ballistic missile submarines, the Land-based Prototype Refueling Overhaul, and the recapitalization of NR's spent fuel handling infrastructure.

Leading Global Partners on Nonproliferation

This Budget Request includes funding to complete the President's four-year pledge in Prague to secure vulnerable nuclear materials. With this Request, the United States will ensure its goals in support of this pledge are completed by December 2013. By the end of 2013, NNSA will have led the effort to remove or dispose of 4,353 kilograms of vulnerable nuclear material (highly enriched uranium (HEU) and plutonium (Pu)) in foreign countries and complete security upgrades on 229 buildings containing weapons-usable nuclear material in the former Soviet Union (FSU).

- As of the end of FY 2012, NNSA's Global Threat Reduction Initiative (GTRI) removed 3,462 kgs of vulnerable nuclear material (HEU/Pu) to secure locations, provided security upgrades to global nuclear and radiological facilities, and converted research reactors to use non-weapons-usable fuel. Through FY 2013, GTRI will have converted or verified as shutdown 88 research reactors, removed 3,835 kilograms of vulnerable nuclear material, and secured an estimated 1,603 buildings containing high priority nuclear or radiological materials.

- As of the end of FY 2012, NNSA's International Material Protection and Cooperation (IMPC) program had secured 218 buildings containing weapons-usable nuclear material to reduce the threat of nuclear terrorism. Through FY 2013 IMPC will have completed nuclear security upgrades at 229 buildings containing weapons-usable nuclear material in the FSU.

Preventing the Proliferation of Nuclear Material and Weapons

The FY 2014 Request for Defense Nuclear Nonproliferation (DNN) is $2.1 billion. The Request funds Administration priorities to develop and implement policy and technical solutions to secure or eliminate proliferation-sensitive materials; limit or prevent the spread of materials, technology, and expertise related to nuclear and radiological weapons and programs around the world; and respond to nuclear incidents. This Budget will enable the United States to complete efforts to secure the most vulnerable nuclear materials by December 2013 and support efforts to design new technologies in support of treaty monitoring and verification, which will contribute to implementation of New START. The Request also broadens cooperative nonproliferation initiatives with foreign governments and international organizations in support of the President's objective of a world without nuclear weapons. The Request also provides funding for NNSA to respond to nuclear or radiological incidents worldwide while advancing our nuclear counterterrorism and counter-proliferation goals through innovative science, technology, and policy-driven solutions.

Decreases to DNN funding are due to the planned December 2013 completion of the domestic uranium enrichment research, development, and demonstration project, and from reassessing the plutonium disposition program. The plutonium disposition program has been building the Mixed Oxide (MOX) Fuel Fabrication Facility in South Carolina to enable DOE to dispose of plutonium by converting it to MOX fuel and burning it in commercial nuclear reactors. This current plutonium disposition approach is facing cost and schedule pressures and the Administration will assess the feasibility of alternative plutonium disposition strategies, resulting in a slowdown of MOX Fuel Fabrication Facility construction in 2014. Nonetheless, the Administration is committed to the overarching goals of the plutonium disposition program to: 1) dispose of excess U.S. weapons plutonium; and 2) achieve Russian disposition of equal quantities of plutonium. The Administration recognizes the importance of the U.S.-Russia Plutonium Management and Disposition Agreement (PMDA), whereby each side committed to dispose of at least 34 metric tons of weapons-grade plutonium.

The FY 2014 Request for the Office of the Administrator (OA) is $398 million. OA provides the Federal salaries and other expenses of the NNSA mission and mission support staff, including the Federal personnel for Defense Programs, Defense Nuclear Nonproliferation, Emergency Operations, Defense Nuclear Security, Acquisition and Project Management, the Office of the NNSA Chief Information Officer, Safety and Health, the Administrator's direct staff, and Federal employees at the Albuquerque Complex and site offices. The Office of the Administrator creates a well-managed, inclusive, responsive, and accountable organization through the strategic management of human capital and greater integration of budget and performance data.

Environmental Management: Advancing Responsible Environmental Cleanup

The mission of the Office of Environmental Management (EM) is to complete the safe cleanup of the environmental legacy brought about from over six decades of nuclear weapons development, production, and Government-sponsored nuclear energy research. This cleanup effort is the largest in the world, originally involving two million acres at 107 sites in 35 states, dealing with some of the most dangerous materials known to human beings. The FY 2014 Budget includes $5.6 billion for EM to protect public health and safety and the environment.

EM continues to pursue its cleanup objectives within the overall framework of achieving the greatest comparative risk reduction benefit and overlaying regulatory compliance commitments and best business practices to maximize cleanup progress. To support this approach, EM has prioritized its cleanup activities:

- Maintain a safe and secure posture in the EM complex
- Radioactive tank waste stabilization, treatment, and disposal
- Spent nuclear fuel storage, receipt, and disposition
- Special nuclear material consolidation, processing, and disposition
- High priority groundwater remediation
- Transuranic and mixed/low-level waste disposition
- Soil and groundwater remediation
- Excess facilities deactivation and decommissioning

The FY 2014 Budget Request will fund activities to maintain a safe and secure posture in the EM complex and positions EM to meet its FY 2014 enforceable agreement milestones. EM

Environmental Management Progress

In FY 2012, the Environmental Management (EM) program made significant progress towards cleaning up Cold War legacy environmental contamination. EM funded cleanup work at 17 sites in 11 states. The EM program is tasked with cleaning up some of the most dangerous materials in the world, and continued progress cleaning up facilities, land and water resources to protect human health and the environment. The FY 2014 EM Budget Request of $5.622 billion enables the program to continue this progress.

Key EM accomplishments in FY 2012 included:

- Cleanup progress

  ✓ EM packaged a record high of 276 canisters of high level waste at the Defense Waste Processing Facility and successfully closed two waste tanks – the first since 1997 – at the Savannah River Site and met the FY 2013 Federal Facilities Agreement tank closure commitment.

  ✓ EM completed the F Reactor Area cleanup at Hanford in July 2012, leaving only the cocooned F Reactor facility standing.

  ✓ In Oak Ridge, EM completed demolition of the North Tower of the K-25 uranium processing facility.

- Contract and project management

  ✓ GAO recognized EM's improvements in contract and project management in its February 2013 update of the high risk list,

  ✓ GAO narrowed the scope of its high risk designation, focusing on EM capital asset projects with costs greater than $750 million.

continues to reduce the greatest risks to the environment and public health, invest in science and technology to reduce lifecycle costs, and make progress towards the goal of reducing EM's geographic footprint 90 percent by 2015. EM will develop new processes to enhance the capability for the disposition of tank waste, nuclear material, and spent (used) nuclear fuel. The FY 2014 Budget Request includes the construction of two unique and complex tank waste processing plants and the operation of another facility to treat approximately 88 million gallons of radioactive tank waste for ultimate disposal. It will also fund the solid waste disposal infrastructure needed to support disposal of transuranic and low-level wastes generated by EM cleanup activities.

As the Department continues to make progress in environmental cleanup, the FY 2014 Budget Request of $177 million for the Office of Legacy Management supports the Department's long-term stewardship responsibilities and payment of pensions and benefits for former contractor workers after site closure. Post closure stewardship includes long-term surveillance and maintenance activities such as groundwater monitoring, disposal cell maintenance, records management, and management of natural resources at sites where active remediation has been completed. Legacy related costs also include the administration of pension and post-retirement benefits for contractor retirees.

Making Progress toward Securing the Long Term Disposal of Nuclear Waste
In 2010, the Administration determined that Yucca Mountain was not a workable solution for disposing of the nation's spent nuclear fuel and high level radioactive waste. The Secretary of Energy established the Blue Ribbon Commission on America's Nuclear Future to review options for managing these wastes and the Commission released its final report in January 2012. After careful consideration of the Commission's recommendations, the Administration released its Strategy for the Management and Disposal of Used Nuclear Fuel and High Level Radioactive Waste in January 2013. The Administration's Strategy supports the principles of the Commission's recommendations and provides a framework for an integrated program for nuclear waste management, including sustainable funding mechanisms. Fundamentals of the Strategy include the creation of a well-defined consent-based facility siting process, implementation of interim storage in the near-term, development of geologic disposal as a permanent solution, establishment of a new body to run the program, and an approach to make funds collected to support nuclear waste management more directly available for that purpose. The Budget provides $60 million for activities to lay the ground work for the design of an integrated waste management system and related research and development activities.

Department of Energy Budget by Organization

	FY 2012 Current	FY 2013 Annualized CR	FY 2014 Request	FY 2014 vs. FY 2012	
				$	%
National Security					
Weapons Activities*	7,214,834	7,557,342	7,868,409	+311,067	+4.1%
Defense Nuclear Nonproliferation	2,300,950	2,409,930	2,140,142	-160,808	-7.0%
Naval Reactors	1,080,000	1,086,610	1,246,134	+166,134	+15.4%
Office of the Administrator	410,000	412,509	397,784	-12,216	-3.0%
Total, National Nuclear Security Administration	*11,005,784*	*11,466,391*	*11,652,469*	*+304,177*	*+2.8%*
Energy and Environment					
Energy Efficiency and Renewable Energy	1,780,548	1,820,713	2,775,700	+995,152	+55.9%
Electricity Delivery and Energy Reliability	136,178	139,954	169,015	+32,837	+24.1%
Fossil Energy	554,806	714,033	637,975	+83,169	+15.0%
Nuclear Energy	853,816	863,996	735,460	-118,356	-13.9%
Race to the Top for Energy Efficiency and Grid Modernization	0	0	200,000	+200,000	N/A
Total, Energy	*3,325,348*	*3,538,696*	*4,518,150*	*+1,192,802*	*+35.9%*
Environment					
Environmental Management	5,710,408	5,745,384	5,621,688	-88,720	-1.6%
Office of Legacy Management	169,600	170,638	176,983	+7,383	+4.4%
Total, Environment	*5,880,008*	*5,916,022*	*5,798,671*	*-81,337*	*-1.4%*
Total, Energy and Environment	**9,205,356**	**9,454,718**	**10,316,821**	**+1,111,465**	**+12.1%**
Science	4,934,980	4,903,461	5,152,752	+217,772	+4.4%
Advanced Research Projects Agency - Energy	275,000	276,683	379,000	+104,000	+37.8%
Corporate Management					
Office of the Secretary	5,030	5,061	5,008	-22	-0.4%
Cost of Work and Revenues	-63,086	-63,472	-59,651	+3,435	+5.4%
Chief Information Officer	84,628	86,454	79,857	-4,771	-5.6%
Chief Financial Officer	53,204	53,530	51,204	-2,000	-3.8%
Management	61,993	63,077	55,699	-6,294	-10.2%
Human Resources	25,089	23,230	24,488	-601	-2.4%
Hearings and Appeals	4,142	4,167	5,022	+880	+21.2%
Congressional and Intergovernmental Affairs	4,690	4,719	4,700	+10	+0.2%
Public Affairs	3,801	3,824	3,597	-204	-5.4%
Office of Indian Energy Policy and Programs	2,000	2,012	2,506	+506	+25.3%
General Counsel	33,053	33,255	33,053	0	N/A
Policy and International Affairs	26,961	27,126	26,961	0	N/A
Economic Impact and Diversity	7,473	7,519	9,806	+2,333	+31.2%
Total, Corporate Management	*248,978*	*250,502*	*242,250*	*-6,728*	*-2.7%*
Credit Programs					
Innovative Technology Loan Guarantee Program	0	0	0	0	N/A
Advanced Technology Vehicles Manufacturing Loan Program	6,000	6,037	6,000	0	N/A
Total, Credit Programs	*6,000*	*6,037*	*6,000*	*0*	*N/A*
Health, Safety and Security	250,737	252,271	251,917	+1,180	+0.5%
Specialized Security Activities	186,699	187,842	196,322	+9,623	+5.2%
Energy Information Administration	105,000	105,643	117,000	+12,000	+11.4%
Inspector General	42,000	42,257	42,120	+120	+0.3%
Power Marketing Administrations	85,090	85,601	85,242	+152	+0.2%
Federal Energy Regulatory Commission	-25,534	-27,479	-26,236	-702	-2.7%
Total, Discretionary Funding by Organization	**26,320,090**	**27,003,927**	**28,415,657**	**+1,753,059**	**+6.7%**

Note: For Weapons Activities, the FY 2014 Request is compared against the FY 2013 Annualized Continuing Resolution level.

Department of Energy Budget by Appropriation

		(discretionary dollars in thousands)			
	FY 2012 Current	FY 2013 Annualized CR	FY 2014 Request	FY 2014 vs. FY 2012	
				$	%
Energy And Water Development, And Related Agencies					
Energy Programs					
Energy Efficiency and Renewable Energy	1,780,548	1,820,713	2,775,700	+995,152	+55.9%
Electricity Delivery and Energy Reliability	136,178	139,954	169,015	+32,837	+24.1%
Nuclear Energy	760,466	770,075	735,460	-25,006	-3.3%
Race to the Top for Energy Efficiency and Grid Modernization	0	0	200,000	+200,000	N/A
Fossil Energy Programs					
Fossil Energy Research and Development	337,074	494,969	420,575	+83,501	+24.8%
Naval Petroleum and Oil Shale Reserves	14,909	15,000	20,000	+5,091	+34.1%
Strategic Petroleum Reserve	192,704	193,883	189,400	-3,304	-1.7%
Northeast Home Heating Oil Reserve	10,119	10,181	8,000	-2,119	-20.9%
Subtotal, Fossil Energy Programs	*554,806*	*714,033*	*637,975*	*+83,169*	*+15.0%*
Uranium Enrichment D&D Fund	472,180	475,070	554,823	+82,643	+17.5%
Energy Information Administration	105,000	105,643	117,000	+12,000	+11.4%
Non-Defense Environmental Cleanup	235,381	236,746	212,956	-22,425	-9.5%
Science	4,934,980	4,903,461	5,152,752	+217,772	+4.4%
Advanced Research Projects Agency - Energy	275,000	276,683	379,000	+104,000	+37.8%
Departmental Administration	126,000	126,772	118,392	-7,608	-6.0%
Inspector General	42,000	42,257	42,120	+120	+0.3%
Innovative Technology Loan Guarantee Program	0	0	0	0	N/A
Advanced Technology Vehicles Manufacturing Loan Program	6,000	6,037	6,000	0	N/A
Total, Energy Programs	**9,428,539**	**9,617,444**	**11,101,193**	**+1,672,654**	**+17.7%**
Atomic Energy Defense Activities					
National Nuclear Security Administration:					
Weapons Activities*	7,214,834	7,557,342	7,868,409	+311,067	+4.1%
Defense Nuclear Nonproliferation	2,300,950	2,409,930	2,140,142	-160,808	-7.0%
Naval Reactors	1,080,000	1,086,610	1,246,134	+166,134	+15.4%
Office of the Administrator	410,000	412,509	397,784	-12,216	-3.0%
Total, National Nuclear Security Administration	*11,005,784*	*11,466,391*	*11,652,469*	*+304,177*	*+2.8%*
Environmental and Other Defense Activities					
Defense Environmental Cleanup	5,002,847	5,033,568	5,316,909	+314,062	+6.3%
Other Defense Activities	823,364	828,402	749,080	-74,284	-9.0%
Total, Environmental & Other Defense Activities	*5,826,211*	*5,861,970*	*6,065,989*	*+239,778*	*+4.1%*
Total, Atomic Energy Defense Activities	*16,831,995*	*17,328,361*	*17,718,458*	*+543,955*	*+3.2%*
Power Marketing Administration					
Southeastern Power Administration	0	0	0	0	N/A
Southwestern Power Administration	11,892	11,965	11,892	0	N/A
Western Area Power Administration	95,978	96,556	95,930	-48	-0.1%
Falcon & Amistad Operating & Maintenance Fund	220	221	420	+200	+90.9%
Colorado River Basins	-23,000	-23,141	-23,000	0	N/A
Transmission Infrastructure Program	0	0	0	0	N/A
Total, Power Marketing Administrations	*85,090*	*85,601*	*85,242*	*+152*	*+0.2%*
Subtotal, Energy And Water Development and Related Agencies	*26,345,624*	*27,031,406*	*28,904,893*	*+2,216,761*	*+8.4%*
Uranium Enrichment D&D (UED&D) Fund Discretionary	0	0	-463,000	-463,000	N/A
Excess Fees and Recoveries, FERC	-25,534	-27,479	-26,236	-702	-2.7%
Total, Discretionary Funding by Appropriation	**26,320,090**	**27,003,927**	**28,415,657**	**+1,753,059**	**+6.7%**

Note: For Weapons Activities, the FY 2014 Request is compared against the FY 2013 Annualized Continuing Resolution level.

	(discretionary dollars in thousands)				
	FY 2014 Request	FY 2015 Request*	FY 2016 Request*	FY 2017 Request*	FY 2018 Request*
Energy And Water Development, And Related Agencies					
Energy Programs					
Energy Efficiency and Renewable Energy	2,775,700	2,848,000	2,904,000	2,967,000	3,034,000
Electricity Delivery and Energy Reliability	169,015	174,000	178,000	182,000	185,000
Nuclear Energy	735,460	843,000	937,000	953,000	971,000
Race to the Top for Energy Efficiency and Grid Modernization	200,000	205,000	209,000	214,000	219,000
Fossil Energy Programs					
Fossil Energy Research and Development	420,575	432,000	440,000	451,000	460,000
Naval Petroleum and Oil Shale Reserves	20,000	21,000	21,000	21,000	22,000
Strategic Petroleum Reserve	189,400	194,000	198,000	202,000	207,000
Northeast Home Heating Oil Reserve	8,000	8,000	8,000	9,000	9,000
Subtotal, Fossil Energy Programs	*637,975*	*655,000*	*667,000*	*683,000*	*698,000*
Uranium Enrichment D&D Fund	554,823	570,000	581,000	593,000	606,000
Energy Information Administration	117,000	120,000	122,000	125,000	128,000
Non-Defense Environmental Cleanup	212,956	217,000	221,000	226,000	232,000
Science	5,152,752	5,289,000	5,390,000	5,509,000	5,630,000
Advanced Research Projects Agency - Energy	379,000	389,000	397,000	405,000	414,000
Departmental Administration	118,392	121,000	124,000	125,000	129,000
Inspector General	42,120	43,000	44,000	45,000	46,000
Innovative Technology Loan Guarantee Program	0	0	0	0	0
Advanced Technology Vehicles Manufacturing Loan Program	6,000	6,000	6,000	6,000	7,000
Total, Energy Programs	*11,101,193*	*11,480,000*	*11,780,000*	*12,033,000*	*12,299,000*
Atomic Energy Defense Activities					
National Nuclear Security Administration:					
Weapons Activities	7,868,409	8,549,698	8,785,395	8,932,772	9,292,929
Defense Nuclear Nonproliferation	2,140,142	1,856,416	1,942,758	2,007,664	1,997,171
Naval Reactors	1,246,134	1,377,100	1,464,600	1,645,463	1,595,416
Office of the Administrator	397,784	407,134	416,706	426,506	436,540
Total, National Nuclear Security Administration	*11,652,469*	*12,190,348*	*12,609,459*	*13,012,405*	*13,322,056*
Environmental and Other Defense Activities					
Defense Environmental Cleanup	5,316,909	5,457,000	5,563,000	5,684,000	5,810,000
Other Defense Activities	749,080	768,000	783,000	801,000	819,000
Total, Environmental & Other Defense Activities	*6,065,989*	*6,225,000*	*6,346,000*	*6,485,000*	*6,629,000*
Total, Atomic Energy Defense Activities	*17,718,458*	*18,415,348*	*18,955,459*	*19,497,405*	*19,951,056*
Power Marketing Administration					
Southeastern Power Administration	0	0	0	0	0
Southwestern Power Administration	11,892	12,000	13,000	14,000	12,000
Western Area Power Administration	95,930	99,000	101,000	103,000	105,000
Falcon & Amistad Operating & Maintenance Fund	420	0	0	0	0
Colorado River Basins	-23,000	-23,000	-24,000	-25,000	-25,000
Transmission Infrastructure Program	0	0	0	0	0
Total, Power Marketing Administrations	*85,242*	*88,000*	*90,000*	*92,000*	*92,000*
Subtotal, Energy And Water Development and Related Agencies	*28,904,893*	*29,983,348*	*30,825,459*	*31,622,405*	*32,342,056*
Uranium Enrichment D&D (UED&D) Fund Discretionary	-463,000	-473,000	-484,000	-494,000	-505,000
Excess Fees and Recoveries, FERC	-26,236	-27,000	-27,000	-28,000	-28,000
Total, Discretionary Funding by Appropriation	**28,415,657**	**29,483,348**	**30,314,459**	**31,100,405**	**31,809,056**

Note: Outyear estimates are largely formulaic estimates by agency for illustrative purposes but they do not reflect final policy levels for those years. Discretionary spending is decided one year at a time and detailed, policy levels for 2015 and beyond will be determined in the context of that President's Budget. The annual totals include an allocation to NNSA from the Department of Defense. The amounts included are $1,196,415 in FY 2015; $1,443,742 in FY 2016; $1,602,266 in FY 2017; and $1,664,372 in FY 2018.

National Nuclear Security Administration

	FY 2012 Current	FY 2013 Annualized CR	FY 2014 Request	FY 2014 vs. FY 2012 (discretionary dollars in thousands)	
				$	%
Weapons Activities*	7,214,834	7,557,342	7,868,409	+311,067	+4.1%
Defense Nuclear Nonproliferation	2,300,950	2,409,930	2,140,142	-160,808	-7.0%
Naval Reactors	1,080,000	1,086,610	1,246,134	+166,134	+15.4%
Office of the Administrator	410,000	412,509	397,784	-12,216	-3.0%
Total, National Nuclear Security Administration	**11,005,784**	**11,466,391**	**11,652,469**	**+304,177**	**+2.8%**

Note: For Weapons Activities, the FY 2014 Request is compared against the FY 2013 Annualized Continuing Resolution level.

The **National Nuclear Security Administration (NNSA)** is critical to ensuring the security and safety of our nation. The NNSA implements programs for four major national security endeavors: leveraging science to maintain a safe, secure, and effective arsenal of nuclear weapons and capabilities to deter any adversary and guarantee that defense to our allies; pursuing our efforts at home and around the world to reduce the global threat posed by nuclear weapons, nuclear proliferation, nuclear terrorism, and unsecured or excess nuclear materials; and providing safe and effective nuclear propulsion for the U.S. Navy.

The **Weapons Activities** FY 2014 Budget Request reflects an increase to meet the Administration's commitments to the programs and capabilities required to maintain a safe, secure, and effective nuclear stockpile. Increases are requested for Directed Stockpile Work for the B61 life extension program and the W78/88-1 life extension study, as well as for Site Stewardship and Nuclear Programs (a new program) to ensure the infrastructure is in place to execute the program mission. The **Defense Nuclear Nonproliferation** FY 2014 Budget Request is driven by the imperative for U.S. leadership in nonproliferation initiatives both here and abroad. Emphasis continues to be on efforts to secure vulnerable nuclear materials around the world while sustaining the capabilities to understand and respond to a wide array of nuclear threats. The **Naval Reactors** FY 2014 Budget Request reflects continued support for the Navy's fleet of nuclear-powered aircraft carriers and submarines as well as three major projects (i.e., OHIO Replacement, Land-based Prototype Refueling Overhaul, and Spent Fuel Handling Recapitalization) which are needed to deliver Navy-established mission requirements. For **Office of the Administrator,** the FY 2014 Budget Request supports the staffing and Federal support needed to meet requirements in the programs.

The FY 2014 Budget Request for the NNSA reflects the importance of the Presidential priorities in meeting the objectives of the Nuclear Posture Review, cooperative global nuclear nonproliferation, modernization of the nuclear complex, and the reactor design and development activities for the Navy's nuclear fleet. NNSA is a key player in the implementation of the President's vision to reduce the role of nuclear weapons in U.S. national security strategy. NNSA will further this goal by maintaining a safe, secure, and effective arsenal to deter any adversary as long as nuclear weapons exist.

	FY 2012 Current	FY 2013 Annualized CR	FY 2014 Request	FY 2014 vs. FY 2013 (discretionary dollars in thousands)	
				$	%
Directed Stockpile Work	1,862,113	2,111,274	2,428,516	+317,242	+15.0%
Science Campaign	331,860	350,104	397,902	+47,798	+13.7%
Engineering Campaign	141,803	150,571	149,911	-660	-0.4%
Inertial Confinement Fusion Ignition and High Yield Campaign	474,484	465,000	401,043	-63,957	-13.8%
Advanced Simulation and Computing Campaign	617,959	595,000	564,329	-30,671	-5.2%
Readiness Campaign	128,406	130,095	197,780	+67,685	+52.0%
Readiness in Technical Base and Facilities	2,013,742	2,216,828	0	-2,216,828	-100.0%
Nuclear Programs	0	0	744,450	+744,450	N/A
Secure Transportation Asset	243,116	219,361	219,190	-171	-0.1%
Nuclear Counterterrorism Incident Response	221,369	247,552	0	-247,552	-100.0%
Facilities and Infrastructure Recapitalization Program	96,120	0	0	0	N/A
Site Stewardship	82,181	90,001	1,706,007	+1,616,006	+1,795.5%
Defense Nuclear Security	692,079	674,504	678,981	+4,477	+0.7%
Cyber Security	131,370	137,022	0	-137,022	-100.0%
NNSA CIO Activities	0	0	148,441	+148,441	N/A
Legacy Contractor Pensions	168,232	185,000	279,597	+94,597	+51.1%
National Security Applications	10,000	18,248	0	-18,248	-100.0%
Subtotal, Weapon Activities	*7,214,834*	*7,590,560*	*7,916,147*	*+325,587*	*+4.3%*
Adjustments	0	-33,218	-47,738	-14,520	-43.7%
Total, Weapons Activities	**7,214,834**	**7,557,342**	**7,868,409**	**+311,067**	**+4.1%**

Note: For Weapons Activities, the FY 2014 Request is compared against the FY 2013 Annualized Continuing Resolution level.

One of the statutory missions of the National Nuclear Security Administration (NNSA) is to maintain and enhance the safety, security, and reliability of the U.S. nuclear weapons stockpile to meet national security requirements. The mission is carried out in partnership with the Department of Defense (DoD), with NNSA providing research, development, and production activities supporting the U.S. nuclear weapons stockpile.

The main components of the Weapons Activities FY 2014 Budget Request are listed below. Program Direction activities, except for Secure Transportation Asset, are funded in a separate appropriation under the Office of the Administrator account.

- **Directed Stockpile Work ($2,428.5 million)**
  Directed Stockpile Work (DSW) activities provide for the Stockpile Management program that ensures the operational readiness of the nuclear weapons in the nation's stockpile through maintenance, surveillance, evaluation, refurbishment, reliability assessment, weapon dismantlement and disposal, research, development, and certification activities. The FY 2014 Budget Request is organized by Life Extension Programs (LEPs) and Major Alterations, Stockpile Systems, Weapons Dismantlement and Disposition, and Stockpile Services.

- **Campaigns ($1,711.0 million)**
  Campaigns are activities which focus on maintaining capabilities to support the scientific and technical efforts essential for the assessment, certification, maintenance, and life extension of the stockpile. The NNSA supports the science, technology and engineering required to maintain a safe, secure and effective stockpile without underground nuclear testing. These dual goals are accomplished by the NNSA pursuing a "science-based" certification and assessments process which relies on surveillance, experiments, modeling, simulation, and historical test data. The Science Campaign develops and applies improved capabilities to assess the safety, reliability, and performance of the nuclear package portion of weapons without further underground

nuclear testing. The Engineering Campaign develops capabilities to assess and improve the safety, reliability, and performance of the non-nuclear and nuclear explosive package engineering components in nuclear weapons. The Inertial Confinement Fusion Ignition and High Yield Campaign develops laboratory capabilities to create and measure thermonuclear ignition, which is expected to provide critical scientific data to support the stockpile without underground nuclear testing. The Advanced Simulation and Computing Campaign provides leading edge, high-end simulation capabilities to meet weapons assessment and certification requirements, including weapon codes, weapons science, platforms, and computer facilities. The Readiness Campaign has the responsibility for development and deployment of modern manufacturing capabilities to produce materials and components in compliance with weapon design and performance requirements, and in accordance with LEPs and refurbishment schedules. It also produces the tritium requirement for the stockpile.

- **Infrastructure and Operations**
  This is a newly created Office (NA-00), that moves NNSA towards a tenant-landlord site model in which NA-00 is the landlord and the Office of Defense Programs is now a tenant. As a result of this reorganization, NNSA is proposing to eliminate the Readiness in Technical Base and Facilities (RTBF) GPRA unit and split these activities between the existing Site Stewardship GPRA unit, and a new GPRA unit titled "Nuclear Programs." The activities managed by NA-00 would be added to Site Stewardship under a new subprogram titled "Enterprise Infrastructure" which would encompass Site Operations, Site Support, Sustainment, Facilities Disposition, and construction. The Nuclear Programs GPRA unit would include program-owned Special Nuclear Materials (SNM) and the execution of investments in enduring DP capabilities into Nuclear Programs.

  o **Nuclear Programs ($744.5 million)** provides mission-essential functions with a focus on Special Nuclear Material (SNM) processing, inventory management, and capability investments. Beginning in Fiscal Year 2014, Nuclear Programs is compromised of three subprogram elements; Nuclear Operations Capability, containing the Program Readiness, Material Recycle and Recovery, and Storage subprograms, all of which were formerly part of Readiness in Technical Base and Facilities, and Plutonium Metal Processing; Capabilities Based Investments and Construction. Nuclear Programs accomplishes its mission by supplying required quantities of program nuclear materials for immediate production use and reserve use in strategic inventories; recovering, recycling, and storing nuclear and select non-nuclear program materials; developing and executing SNM strategies for Defense Programs operations; sustaining program skills through personnel training and development; developing and operating SNM processing technology improvements and functionality; and managing capability investments and line-item construction projects.

  o **Site Stewardship ($1,706.0 million)** ensures the overall health and viability of NNSA's nuclear security enterprise and brings focus to long term sustainment of its facilities and infrastructure, stabilization, consolidation, packaging, and disposition of nuclear materials. It also focuses on the operation and maintenance of the Nuclear Materials Management and Safeguards System that is used to track and account for nuclear materials at DOE and the Nuclear Regulatory Commission licensed sites and the standardization of NNSA project management processes. In addition, the Enterprise Infrastructure (EI) subprogram will provide an enterprise-wide look and a renewed prioritization strategy for all nuclear security infrastructure customers without sacrificing needed infrastructure investments for short term programmatic needs. The EI subprogram will also provide safe, secure, and compliant facilities and infrastructure to support national security mission needs of the NNSA.

- **Secure Transportation Asset ($219.2 million)**
  This program provides for the safe, secure movement of nuclear weapons, special nuclear materials, and weapon components to meet projected DOE and DoD requirements. The Program Direction in this account provides for the secure transportation workforce which includes Federal Agents.

- **Defense Nuclear Security ($679.0 million)**
  This program provides protection for NNSA personnel, facilities, nuclear weapons and information from a full spectrum of threats, most notably from terrorism attacks in the United States.

- **NNSA CIO Activities ($148.4 million)**
  This program supports the diverse civilian nuclear security enterprise of the U.S. DOE/NNSA, leading Federal efforts to research and develop information technology and cyber security solutions, including continuous monitoring, enterprise wireless and security technologies (such as: identity, credential, and access management) to help meet energy security, proliferation resistance, and climate goals. Activities previously funded in the Cyber Security program are integrated into the NNSA CIO Activities program in FY 2014.

NNSA's FY 2014 Budget Request continues significant efforts to meet nuclear security priorities, to conduct the **Stockpile Management** program, and to continue leveraging science to enhance national security. The investment strategy in this Request provides a strong basis for transitioning to a smaller nuclear stockpile that continues to be safe, secure and effective. The key stockpile initiatives are continuations of the W76 LEP, the B61 LEP, the W78/88-1 life extension study, and the W88 ALT 370. This Request supports the science, technology and engineering base, and modernizes key nuclear facilities. These investments are critical in order to strengthen the nation's security while supporting a reduced reliance on nuclear weapons and to sustain confidence in the ability to certify the without the use of underground nuclear testing. Targeted increases are therefore provided for Stockpile Support; Science, Technology and Engineering; and Infrastructure.

The increase in **Stockpile Support** provides for the Stockpile Management program and reflects the ramp up of Phase 6.3 activities for the B61 LEP, W78/88-1 Study activities, and an increase for current systems, including maintenance (neutron generator activities), surveillance, and W88 ALT 370 arming, fuzing, and firing set development efforts.

The sustained support for **Science, Technology and Engineering** is crucial to provide the technical and scientific basis to ensure that the nation's nuclear weapons are safe, secure and reliable, without the use of underground nuclear testing. The FY 2014 Budget Request supports the science necessary for certification, including the work toward ignition at the National Ignition Facility, plutonium experiments to evaluate pit reuse for LEPs, and the computational and simulation capability which are essential to supporting the stockpile.

Infrastructure and **Construction** support in the Request is targeted toward maintaining and improving current infrastructure and support, and construction of replacement uranium manufacturing and waste facilities.

The **Defense Nuclear Security** and **NNSA CIO Activities** budgets continue to provide protection in the areas of physical and cyber security from a full spectrum of threats. The physical security budget is based on risk-informed decisions and is fully consistent with the Department's Graded Security Protection policy. The increase in the NCIO budget reflects the current total cost for information technology services, unclassified business operations, and records management support.

Defense Nuclear Nonproliferation – NNSA

	FY 2012 Current*	FY 2013 Annualized CR	FY 2014 Request	FY 2014 vs. FY 2012	
				$	%
Defense Nuclear Nonproliferation Programs					
Global Threat Reduction Initiative	503,453	501,048	424,487	-78,966	-15.7%
Defense Nuclear Nonproliferation R&D	347,905	456,317	388,838	+40,933	11.8%
Nonproliferation and International Security	153,594	154,534	141,675	-11,919	-7.8%
International Material Protection and Cooperation	575,789	573,415	369,625	-206,164	-35.8%
Fissile Materials Disposition	685,386	721,784	502,557	-182,829	-26.7%
Legacy Contractor Pensions	55,823	56,165	93,703	+37,880	67.9%
Subtotal, Defense Nuclear Nonproliferation Programs	*2,321,950*	*2,463,263*	*1,920,885*	*-401,065*	*-17.3%*
Nuclear Counterterrorism Incident Response Program	0	0	181,293	+181,293	N/A
Counterterrorism and Counterproliferation Programs	0	0	74,666	+74,666	N/A
Subtotal, Defense Nuclear Nonproliferation	*2,321,950*	*2,463,263*	*2,176,844*	*-145,106*	*-6.2%*
Adjustments*	-21,000	-53,333	-36,702	-15,702	-74.8%
Total, Defense Nuclear Nonproliferation	**2,300,950**	**2,409,930**	**2,140,142**	**-160,808**	**-7.0%**

(discretionary dollars in thousands)

Note: The FY 2012 Current column includes international contributions and reflects transfers out of the Defense Nuclear Nonproliferation account for Small Business Innovation Research and Small Business Technology Transfer. Adjustments include rescissions and reprogramming of prior year balances.

NNSA's **Defense Nuclear Nonproliferation (DNN)** appropriation has been restructured to include the programs within the Office of Defense Nuclear Nonproliferation (DNN), the Office of Emergency Operations (which manages the Nuclear Counterterrorism Incident Response (NCTIR) program), and the Office of Counterterrorism and Counterproliferation (which manages the Counterterrorism and Counterproliferation (CTCP) Programs). Each office reports directly to the Acting Administrator. These programs provide policy and technical leadership to limit or prevent the spread of nuclear and radiological materials and associated technology and expertise; advance technologies that detect nuclear and radiological proliferation worldwide; eliminate or secure inventories of surplus materials and infrastructure usable for nuclear weapons; and provide the technical capability to understand and respond to incidents worldwide and address the danger that hostile nations or terrorist groups may acquire nuclear or radiological material, dual-use production technology, or expertise.

By drawing together these three NNSA programs, we strengthen the existing synergies and cooperation among these offices. In doing so, we provide priority and emphasis to NNSA programs that are responsible for implementing the President's nuclear security priorities and the 2010 Nuclear Posture Review (NPR) which "outlines the Administration's approach to promoting the President's agenda for reducing nuclear dangers and pursuing the goal of a world without nuclear weapons, while simultaneously advancing broader U.S. security interests." Based on the fundamental and continuing changes in both the domestic and the international security environments, the NPR report identifies preventing nuclear proliferation and nuclear terrorism as the highest of five key areas of focus. This change in budget structure presents with greater clarity the total funding and level of activity undertaken by NNSA in this increasingly important area. At the same time, this realignment ensures that the Weapons Activities appropriation is now entirely focused on the U.S. nuclear stockpile and related activities.

The FY 2014 Budget Request supports national security priorities articulated in the National Security Strategy, and reflected in the Department of Energy and National Nuclear Security Administration Strategic Plans. These priorities include the four-year effort to secure or eliminate the world's most vulnerable nuclear weapon materials; disposing of excess nuclear weapon materials in the United States; supporting the development of new technologies for nonproliferation; promoting the secure expansion of nuclear energy; and improving capabilities worldwide to deter and detect the illicit movement of nuclear and radiological materials.

Excluding the additions of NCTIR and CTCP, the DNN FY 2014 Budget Request reduces funding for the five DNN programs by -$416.8 million (-18.1%) from the FY 2012 current level. This decrease is primarily driven by reductions in the Fissile Materials Disposition and International Material Protection and Cooperation programs. Major areas of work include:

- **Global Threat Reduction Initiative ($424.5 million)**
  The Global Threat Reduction Initiative (GTRI) reduces and protects vulnerable nuclear and radiological materials located at civilian sites worldwide. GTRI seeks to prevent terrorists from acquiring nuclear and radiological materials that could be used in weapons or other acts of terrorism by converting research reactors and isotope production facilities from using highly enriched uranium to low enriched uranium (HEU to LEU); removing and disposing of excess nuclear and radiological materials; and protecting high priority nuclear and radiological materials from theft and sabotage.

  GTRI directly supports the international efforts to secure and/or remove the most vulnerable nuclear material within four years, by December 2013. The FY 2014 Budget includes funding to convert or shutdown a cumulative total of 92 HEU Reactors, remove a cumulative total of 4,400 kilograms of vulnerable nuclear material (HEU and plutonium), and protect a cumulative total of 1,708 buildings with high priority nuclear and radiological materials.

- **Defense Nuclear Nonproliferation Research and Development ($388.8 million)**
  Defense Nuclear Nonproliferation Research and Development (DNN R&D) reduces national security threats by developing technical capabilities that improve the detection, identification, and characterization of the full life cycle of foreign nuclear weapons development programs. These include technical capabilities to detect foreign nuclear weapons development, nuclear detonations, and the movement or diversion of special nuclear materials; monitor compliance with nuclear arms control and nonproliferation commitments; discourage the unnecessary spread of enrichment technology; and inform policymakers of current and future technical capabilities available for meeting potential nuclear nonproliferation and arms control treaty objectives. To meet National and Departmental nuclear security requirements, DNN R&D leverages the unique facilities and scientific skills of the NNSA nuclear security enterprise, other DOE national laboratories, academia, and industry.

  The DNN R&D program will continue to advance the state of the art in proliferation detection and nuclear detonation detection capabilities. DNN R&D will expand efforts in nonproliferation and foreign weapons program activity monitoring through continued development of a series of national test beds, including capabilities to detect and identify extremely low-yield nuclear detonations with increasing confidence. DNN R&D will continue to support a complex warhead measurement campaign with NNSA's Defense Programs that, upon completion, will provide a robust basis for demonstrating a weapons and material accountability test bed to define technical limits and opportunities for end-to-end arms control transparency. DNN R&D program will deliver nuclear detonation detection payloads for Global Positioning System (GPS) block III satellites in accordance with negotiated schedule with USAF. It will support the payload-side technical integration, pre-launch and on-orbit testing activities for previously delivered payloads in accordance with host satellite schedules. Finally, DNN R&D will develop treaty monitoring focused payloads and support integration onto its designated satellite and conduct research in seismic, radionuclide and detonation forensics to support national capability in terrestrial and airborne monitoring and analysis methods.

- **Nonproliferation and International Security ($141.7 million)**
  Nonproliferation and International Security (NIS) supports NNSA efforts to prevent the proliferation of nuclear materials, technology, and expertise by states and non-state actors. NIS focuses on strengthening the nonproliferation regime to reduce proliferation by applying its unique policy and technical expertise to safeguard nuclear material and strengthen its physical security; control the spread of nuclear material, equipment, technology, and expertise; verify nuclear reductions and compliance with nonproliferation treaties and agreements; and develop and implement Department of Energy (DOE/NNSA) nonproliferation and arms control policy.

  The NIS FY 2014 Budget Request supports the implementation of the Next Generation Safeguards Initiative to strengthen IAEA safeguards and to revitalize the U.S. technical and human capital base that supports them; efforts to reduce proliferation risks associated with the expansion of nuclear power; and the development and implementation of reliable fuel services as an alternative to the spread of enrichment and reprocessing capabilities. This funding will also support applied development and evaluation of technologies to support U.S. arms control and nonproliferation initiatives, including treaty verification and transparency. Lastly, the funding profile provides for activities that prevent and counter proliferation including continued support of U.S. efforts to address proliferation by Iran, North Korea, and proliferation networks; implement nuclear arms reduction and associated agreements; strengthen international nonproliferation agreements and standards; implement statutory export control and safeguards requirements; encourage global adherence to and implementation of international nonproliferation requirements; and support high priority diplomatic initiatives.

- **International Material Protection and Cooperation ($369.6 million)**
  International Material Protection and Cooperation (IMP&C) works to prevent nuclear terrorism by working in Russia and other regions of concern to secure and eliminate vulnerable nuclear weapons and weapons-usable material under the Material Protection, Control and Accounting (MPC&A) Program. IMP&C also installs and sustains detection equipment under the Second Line of Defense Program at international border crossings and major seaports to prevent illicit transfer of nuclear material.

  The International Material Protection and Cooperation program will complete MPC&A upgrades in Russia on approximately 229 buildings containing weapons usable nuclear material by the end of calendar-year 2013; blend-down a total of approximately 16.8 MTs of HEU by the end of FY 2014; and complete installation of detection equipment at a cumulative total of 538 SLD sites in FY 2014.

- **Fissile Materials Disposition ($502.6 million)**
  Fissile Materials Disposition (FMD) conducts activities in the United States to dispose of surplus weapon-grade fissile materials, and supports disposal of Russian surplus weapon-grade plutonium. The program also supports the international discussion on management and disposition of plutonium.

  The Fissile Materials Disposition program is vital to the nation's arms control and nuclear nonproliferation efforts. NNSA remains committed to plutonium disposition but has begun assessing alternative plutonium disposition strategies in FY 2013 and will identify options for FY 2014. FMD will continue to engage with its Russian counterparts during this assessment.

- **Nuclear Counterterrorism Incident Response ($181.3 million)**
  The Nuclear Counterterrorism Incident Response (NCTIR) program, previously funded in the Weapons Activities appropriation, applies technical assets from the nuclear security enterprise to resolve or manage nuclear and radiological incidents, especially those involving terrorism. NCTIR maintains essential components of the nation's capability to respond to and manage the consequences domestically or internationally of civilian radiation exposure resulting from an attack. NCTIR integrates NNSA expertise with

law enforcement and military capabilities to locate, identify, and disable a terrorist nuclear device, and manages the effects of an attack by collaborating with federal, state, and local emergency management organizations. NCTIR contributes to the response capability by maintaining response teams comprised of technical specialists and conducting programs to train and equip response organizations on the technical aspects of nuclear counterterrorism.

The FY 2014 Budget Request for NCTIR will support a strategy focused on readiness to help NNSA achieve the stated goals. This strategy supports reducing nuclear dangers through integration of its Emergency Management, Emergency Response, Forensics and International activities supported by training and operations.

- **Counterterrorism and Counterproliferation Programs ($74.7 million)**
  The Counterterrorism and Counterproliferation (CTCP) Programs advance U.S. Government counterterrorism and counterproliferation goals through innovative science, technology, and policy-driven solutions. CTCP consolidates activities previously conducted under the Nuclear Counterterrorism subprogram of NCTIR and the National Security Applications program (both previously funded in the Weapons Activities appropriation) into an integrated program of technical work that materially contributes to the Department's goal of enhancing nuclear security through preventing nuclear terrorism. Funds in this budget primarily will be spent on scientific efforts to understand nuclear threat devices, including improvised nuclear devices, foreign nuclear weapons (with emphasis on loss of custody), and their constituents (namely nuclear and energetic materials). Key CTCP technical activities sustain and exercise the U.S. Government's ability to understand and prevent nuclear terrorism and to counter nuclear device proliferation. Other activities within CTCP include national and international outreach to strengthen nuclear counterterrorism capabilities through table-top exercises, bilateral dialogues, and technical exchanges. Finally, CTCP supports interagency efforts through jointly-coordinated, long-term R&D on selected counterterrorism, survivability, and weapons effects activities and by providing critical technical expertise through details and assignments.

The FY 2014 Budget Request for CTCP supports the President's goal to protect Americans from the danger of nuclear terrorism, the greatest threat to global security. This program provides tremendous return on investment because it leverages the full range of tools, techniques, and expertise developed within the nuclear weapons design and engineering laboratories. While protecting Americans from the threat of nuclear harm, these investments in science and innovation help prevent nuclear terrorism and the proliferation of nuclear material and weapons.

	FY 2012 Current	FY 2013 Annualized CR	FY 2014 Request	FY 2014 vs. FY 2012 (discretionary dollars in thousands)	
				$	%
Naval Reactors Operations and Infrastructure	358,300	360,493	455,740	+97,440	+27.2%
Naval Reactors Development	421,000	423,577	419,400	-1,600	-0.4%
S8G Prototype Refueling	99,500	100,109	144,400	+44,900	+45.1%
OHIO Replacement Reactor Systems Development	121,300	122,042	126,400	+5,100	+4.2%
Program Direction	40,000	40,245	44,404	+4,404	+11.0%
Construction	39,900	40,144	69,773	+29,873	+74.9%
Subtotal, Naval Reactors	*1,080,000*	*1,086,610*	*1,260,117*	*180,117*	*16.7%*
Adjustment	0	0	-13,983	-13,983	N/A
Total, Naval Reactors	**1,080,000**	**1,086,610**	**1,246,134**	**+166,134**	**+15.4%**

The **Naval Reactors** program has responsibility for all naval nuclear propulsion work, beginning with reactor plant technology development and design, continuing through reactor plant operation and maintenance, and ending with reactor plant disposal.

Funding for the program includes day-to-day challenges associated with the safe and reliable operation of the Navy's nuclear-powered fleet (72 submarines and 10 aircraft carriers), constituting over 40% of the Navy's major combatants. The program's development work consists of refining and improving existing technology to ensure that the US Navy's nuclear propulsion plants are increasingly efficient and effective and will be capable of meeting future threats to national security.

In addition to its support to the fleet, Naval Reactors' work includes three major initiatives: the OHIO-class Ballistic Missile Submarine Replacement, Land-based Prototype Refueling Overhaul, and the Spent Fuel Handling Recapitalization Project.

Naval Reactors supports the President's national security strategy with the continued development of the OHIO Replacement submarine and stewardship of naval nuclear infrastructure. Ensuring the continuity of a sea-based strategic deterrent, the Budget Request provides for the research, design, and development of the OHIO Replacement submarine. The budget further provides funding for the refueling and overhaul of the Land-based Prototype reactor, a critical research and development asset for the long-term, as well as for the development of a life-of-ship reactor core for the OHIO Replacement. The Spent Fuel Handling Recapitalization Project will ensure the capability to refuel and defuel aircraft carriers and submarines over the long-term, which is critical to maintaining the nuclear fleet's operational availability for national security missions.

- **Naval Reactors Operations and Infrastructure ($455.7 million)**
  The increase supports deferred work to recapitalize the program's unique infrastructure and enable the program's long-term operation including continued design of the Spent Fuel Handling Recapitalization Project.

- **Naval Reactors Development ($419.4 million)**
  This decrease reflects decreasing requirements for construction support for FORD-class reactor plants and completion of VIRGINIA Forward Fit design.

- **S8G Prototype Refueling ($144.4 million)**
  The increase in S8G Prototype Refueling supports the Land-based Prototype Refueling Overhaul completion in 2021 and is inclusive of development of technology to support the OHIO Replacement Program.

- **OHIO Replacement Reactor Systems Development ($126.4 million)**
  The increase in OHIO Replacement funding supports ongoing reactor design efforts to support long-lead procurements and ship construction beginning in 2021.

- **Construction ($69.8 million)**
  The increase supports line-item funding for the Spent Fuel Handling Recapitalization Project, Remote-Handled Low-Level Waste Disposal Project, the Material Characterization Laboratory at Knolls Atomic Power Laboratory, and the Radiological Work and Storage Building at the Kesselring Site, which is partially offset by decreases in construction funding for the Expended Core Facility M-290 Receiving/Discharge Station.

- **Program Direction ($44.4 million)**
  The change reflects an increase commensurate with the higher costs of qualified and experienced engineering personnel.

	FY 2012 Current	FY 2013 Annualized CR	FY 2014 Request	FY 2014 vs. FY 2012 (discretionary dollars in thousands)	
				$	%
Office of the Administrator	410,000	412,509	397,784	-12,216	-3.0%
Total, Office of the Administrator	**410,000**	**412,509**	**397,784**	**-12,216**	**-3.0%**

NNSA's **Office of the Administrator** FY 2014 Budget Request provides for a well-managed, inclusive, responsive, and accountable organization through the strategic management of human capital and acquisitions and integration of budget and performance data. The workforce is a highly educated and skilled cadre of federal managers who oversee the operations of the nuclear security enterprise and perform many specialized duties including leading emergency response teams, nuclear nonproliferation leadership, safeguards and security oversight, policy and strategic coordination of counterterrorism and counter proliferation initiatives, and mission support to include: procurement, financial management, human capital management, legal services, and safety and health. The Naval Reactors and Secure Transportation Asset programs retain separately funded program direction accounts.

The organizational structure includes seven site offices that oversee NNSA contractor operations located at Lawrence Livermore, Los Alamos, and Sandia National Laboratories; the Pantex and Kansas City Plants; the Y-12 National Security Complex; the Savannah River Site; and the Nevada National Security Site.

This program provides funding for federal staff and required support for NNSA activities at Headquarters and field locations, as well as support for Departmental administrative activities through the Working Capital Fund.

The FY 2014 Budget Request provides support for 1,817 Full-Time Equivalents and other expenses of the Federal staff. The Budget Request reflects several major changes that were identified in the FY 2013 Budget Request, including the functional transfer of Federal Unclassified Information Technology to Weapons Activities and the transfer of overseas office support to the Working Capital Fund (WCF). The budget reflects a significant reduction to NNSA's Program Direction spending, including reductions to Federal staff, travel, and support services. Reductions associated with the transfer of Federal unclassified information technology are largely offset by additional contributions to the WCF.

Energy Efficiency and Renewable Energy

	FY 2012 Current	FY 2013 Annualized CR	FY 2014 Request	FY 2014 vs. FY 2012 (discretionary dollars in thousands)	
				$	%
Vehicle Technologies	320,966	330,819	575,000	+254,034	+79.1%
Bioenergy Technologies	0	0	282,000	+282,000	N/A
Biomass And Biorefinery Systems RD&D	194,995	200,496	0	-194,995	-100.0%
Hydrogen And Fuel Cell Technologies	101,326	104,258	100,000	-1,326	-1.3%
Solar Energy	284,702	290,719	356,500	+71,798	+25.2%
Wind Energy	91,813	93,825	144,000	+52,187	+56.8%
Water Power	58,076	59,147	55,000	-3,076	-5.3%
Geothermal Technology	36,979	38,094	60,000	+23,021	+62.3%
Advanced Manufacturing	0	0	365,000	+365,000	N/A
Industrial Technologies	112,692	116,287	0	-112,692	-100.0%
Federal Energy Management Program	29,891	30,074	36,000	+6,109	+20.4%
Building Technologies	214,706	220,546	300,000	+85,294	+39.7%
Weatherization And Intergovernmental Activities	128,000	128,783	248,000	+120,000	+93.8%
Program Direction	165,000	166,010	185,000	+20,000	+12.1%
Strategic Programs	25,000	25,153	36,000	+11,000	+44.0%
Facilities And Infrastructure	26,311	26,472	46,000	+19,689	+74.8%
Subtotal, Energy Efficiency And Renewable Energy	*1,790,457*	*1,830,683*	*2,788,500*	*998,043*	*+55.7%*
Use of Prior Year Balances and Other Adjustments	-9,909	-9,970	-12,800	-2,891	-29.2%
Total, Energy Efficiency And Renewable Energy	**1,780,548**	**1,820,713**	**2,775,700**	**+995,152**	**+55.9%**

The **Office of Energy Efficiency and Renewable Energy (EERE)** seeks to ensure American leadership in the transition to a global clean energy economy. EERE supports research, development, demonstration, and deployment (RDD&D) through partnerships with some of America's most innovative businesses and research institutions with the explicit goal of making a wide array of clean energy technologies directly cost-competitive, without subsidies, with the conventional energy technologies the Nation uses today. To achieve this, EERE focuses its RDD&D investments on high-impact activities in the areas of sustainable transportation, renewable electricity, and end-use energy efficiency in buildings and factories.

EERE is positioned to achieve its goals through the FY 2014 Budget Request by developing and accelerating the adoption of new energy generation technologies — technologies that will make our buildings, factories, power plants, and vehicles cleaner, safer and more efficient and productive. EERE's work helps ensure that U.S. manufacturers and U.S. workers lead the race for and secure the benefits of a clean, domestically powered energy system as a foundation for a prosperous American future.

EERE prioritizes its RDD&D work according to its "5 Core Questions":
- High Impact: Is this a high-impact problem?
- Additionality: Will the EERE funding make a large difference relative to what the private sector (and other funding entities) is already doing?
- Openness: Has EERE made sure to focus on the broad problem that is being solved and is EERE open to new ideas, new approaches, and new performers?
- Enduring Economic Benefit: How will the EERE funding result in enduring economic benefit to the United States?
- Proper Role of Government: Why is what you are doing a proper high-impact role of government versus something best left to the private sector to address on its own?

Through decades of committed, forward-leaning RDD&D investments, EERE has made tremendous progress toward its goal of making a wide array of clean energy technologies directly cost-competitive with traditional forms of energy without subsidies. Recent noteworthy successes demonstrate the value of our core programs and their ability to achieve results for the Nation. A recent body of impact assessments performed for six specific EERE programs estimates that these programs alone have generated hundreds of billions of dollars in net economic benefits over the past few decades[1].

Representative EERE accomplishments include:

- The investments EERE made in combustion efficiency R&D over the 20-year period from 1986-2007 resulted in $70.2 billion dollars in total economic benefits, along with concomitant health benefits, in the heavy-duty diesel trucking sector, representing a more than 70:1 return on the taxpayer investment. In addition, virtually every hybrid electric vehicle on the road today has EERE-developed technology inside – an improved nickel-metal hydride battery – providing up to a 50% increase in fuel economy compared to non-hybrid vehicles. The U.S. now has more than 2.5 million hybrid electric vehicles on the road today.
- Supported by EERE RD&D investments, the estimated production cost of electric vehicle batteries has been reduced by 50% in just the last four years. Plug-in electric vehicle (PEV) sales increased to more than 50,000 last year, representing a more than tripling of sales year-on-year.
- In 2012, EERE successfully achieved its 10-year goal of demonstrating cellulosic ethanol at the pilot scale at an estimated production-scale cost of $2.15/gallon.
- EERE has supported first-of-a kind integrated biorefineries across the United States through public-private partnerships, the first of which is expected to be operating commercially in 2013.
- EERE's R&D efforts in solar photovoltaics are estimated to have accelerated the solar industry's technological progress by approximately 12 years.

Key strategic areas of focus and selected targets within EERE's technology-specific offices are presented below:
Transportation Goals — Reduce oil net imports in half by 2020.
- Vehicles — FY 2014 funding will support a number of aggressive vehicle technology goals. Increased funding will support the following: Energy Storage, Electric Motor R&D, and Advanced Power Electronics initiatives in support of the EV Everywhere Grand Challenge; initiate research to better integrate electric vehicles, building energy management systems, and solar-generation technologies into the grid distribution system; improvements in lightweight materials performance; enable initiation of Advanced Vehicle Community Partner projects that would test different real-world approaches for increasing advanced vehicle adoption in localities; and provide an incubator program targeting off-roadmap innovation.
- Bioenergy — FY 2014 funding will initiate laboratory-scale proof-of-concept work on novel technologies identified through pathways analysis, including Advanced Technologies for Bioconversion Efficiency, Bio-Oil R&D, and an incubator program targeting off-roadmap innovation. Additionally, as part of EERE's Clean Energy Manufacturing Initiative, the program will invest in R&D for biomass-derived low-cost carbon fiber manufacturing.
- Fuel Cells — FY 2014 funding will support the targeted reduction of the cost of fuel cells from $47/kW (projected cost at high-volume manufacturing) today to $30/kW in 2017, and will improve fuel cell durability from 2,500 hours (equivalent to 75,000 miles) to 5,000 hours (150,000 miles) by 2017.

Renewable Electricity Goals — Double renewable electricity generation from wind, solar and geothermal sources by 2020 (from 2012 levels). Generate 80% of electricity from a diverse set of clean energy sources by 2035.
- Solar – FY 2014 funding will support Sunshot-focused R&D aimed at achieving directly cost-competitive solar power without subsidies by reducing the levelized cost of solar energy to $.06/kWh by 2020. In addition, the Solar program will invest in research to better integrate solar power, electric vehicles, and building energy management systems into the grid distribution system; a cost-shared Utility PV Challenge that will identify

---

[1]   http://www1.eere.energy.gov/analysis/pe_index.html

and demonstrate best practices and new business models to support large amounts of distributed generation; and R&D to address costs associated with Soft Balance of Systems.

- Wind — To be competitive with fossil fuels without subsidies, wind energy R&D efforts must extend into optimizing overall wind-plant performance and operations. The increase in FY 2014 funding meets this challenge by placing a greater focus on wind-plant optimization modeling, including complex flow analysis, component and system design impacts, and test campaigns. It also includes a new initiative on next-generation advanced rotors, including very-large-scale wind rotors suitable for wind environments such as offshore. New initiatives on manufacturing next-generation components and research necessary to overcome permitting challenges will also be supported.

Energy Efficiency Goals – Double American energy productivity by 2030 (from 2010 levels) by reducing the amount of energy used per dollar of Gross Domestic Product (GDP) (energy intensity).

- Advanced Manufacturing Office (AMO) — Additional funding in FY 2014 will support the deployment of three or more Clean Energy Manufacturing Innovation (CEMI) Institutes, consistent with the President's vision for a National Network for Manufacturing Innovation, aimed at bringing together universities, companies, and the Government to co-invest in solving industry-relevant problems. The CEMI Institutes are intended to provide researchers (from small- and medium-sized enterprises and large companies) timely, affordable access to physical and virtual tools, and to demonstrate new materials and critical processes to advance the use of clean energy manufacturing technologies for industry. In addition, AMO will invest in transformational research and development projects focused on foundational manufacturing processes and materials. These projects will address core technical issues for foundational technologies that will enable U.S. manufacturers to realize significant gains in energy productivity, environmental performance, product yield, and economic competitiveness.

In addition to supporting aggressive RDD&D in each of EERE's technology-specific offices, the FY 2014 Budget Request reflects increased focus on high-impact, new cross-cutting efforts that are breaking down the silos between EERE's technology-specific offices. These cross-cutting initiatives include:

- **EV Everywhere Grand Challenge** — a DOE-wide, cross-cutting initiative focused on breakthroughs in plug-in electric vehicle technology to achieve the goal of making the U.S. the first country in the world to invent and produce plug-in electric vehicles that are as affordable and convenient as gasoline-powered vehicles by 2022.
- **Clean Energy Manufacturing Initiative** – a new cross-cutting EERE initiative focused on dramatically improving U.S. competitiveness in the manufacturing of clean energy products (like solar modules, LED's, batteries, and wind blades) and strengthening U.S. competitiveness across multiple manufacturing industries through increased energy productivity.
- **SunShot Grand Challenge** – a DOE-wide initiative focused on achieving directly cost-competitive solar power by 2020.
- **EERE Grid Integration Initiative** — a cross-cutting and integrated initiative in which EERE's vehicles, solar, and buildings programs, working in coordination with DOE's Grid Tech Team, to address grid integration barriers and opportunities associated with variable, distributed renewable energy generators, electric vehicle charging, and building efficiency and controls. These activities seek to develop and validate technologies, tools, and approaches that overcome grid integration barriers associated with EERE technologies, so that key stakeholders achieve the confidence within their risk tolerance necessary to install high penetration of clean energy technologies while maintaining grid reliability.
- **Wide Bandgap Semiconductors for Clean Energy Initiative** — Wide bandgap semiconductor technology, which was initially developed for military and solid-state lighting uses, is a key next-generation platform for semiconductor devices that offers the potential for high-power-conversion electronics that are much more compact and efficient and can operate at much higher temperatures and voltages. This revolutionary technology has the potential to be a platform for the next generation of electric drivetrains, solar inverters,

high-efficiency motors, solid-state transformers for the grid, and many other critical, clean energy applications.

In the current time of fiscal and budget austerity, it is more important, now than ever before, that EERE use the funds made available by the Congress as efficiently and carefully as possible. For this reason, and at the direction of this Committee, starting in FY 2014, EERE will be fully and uniformly implementing Active Project Management, under which every single competitive project awarded going forward will be a cooperative agreement, not a grant, to enable greater EERE oversight; and it will be subject to aggressive, annual go-no go milestones, rigorous quarterly reviews, and early termination in the event of insufficient technical performance. This approach ensures that EERE has the correct tools and oversight over projects to maximize the taxpayer's return on investment.

Electricity Delivery and Energy Reliability

	FY 2012 Current	FY 2013 Annualized CR	FY 2014 Request	FY 2014 vs. FY 2012	
(discretionary dollars in thousands)				$	%
Clean Energy Transmission and Reliability	24,665	25,569	32,000	+7,335	+29.7%
Smart Grid	23,203	24,055	14,400	-8,803	-37.9%
Energy Storage	19,336	20,046	15,000	-4,336	-22.4%
Cybersecurity for Energy Delivery Systems	29,007	30,072	38,000	+8,993	+31.0%
Electricity Systems Hub	0	0	20,000	+20,000	N/A
National Electicity Delivery	6,976	7,019	6,000	-976	-14.0%
Infrastructure Security and Energy Restoration	5,981	6,018	16,000	+10,019	+167.5%
Program Direction	27,010	27,175	27,615	+605	+2.2%
Total, Electricity Delivery And Energy Reliability	**136,178**	**139,954**	**169,015**	**+32,837**	**+24.1%**

The **Office of Electricity Delivery and Energy Reliability (OE)** drives electric grid modernization and resiliency in the energy infrastructure while working to enable innovation across the energy sector, empowering American consumers, and securing our energy future. The OE mission and the leadership role OE plays in the energy industry directly support the President's effort to accelerate the transformation of America's energy system through research and development, partnerships, facilitation, modeling and analytics, and emergency preparedness.

Over the years, major advancements across the energy industry have been made through OE's support. Research investments in cybersecurity have resulted in capabilities that prevent unexpected communications or processes on protected energy system components; these capabilities are expected to become commercially available this year. Longtime support for research, development and deployment of synchrophasors has revolutionized the broader visibility into the condition of the electric grid, providing near real-time data on transmission system conditions that helps grid operators better understand the complexities of a dynamic power system, and therefore reduce the frequency and scope of outages. By investing in efforts that enhance the resiliency of the energy infrastructure, and through OE's role as the energy-sector lead for response and restoration for major disruptions, more U.S. communities have been able to restore power quicker. Through its state technical assistance efforts, OE has developed a modeling tool to help state utility commissions quantitatively evaluate electric utility financial impacts under different energy efficiency scenarios, and has helped states identify ways to better integrate variable generation, such as wind and solar, into the grid.

The FY 2014 Budget Request reflects an increased investment in modernizing the grid and in strengthening the resiliency of the energy infrastructure system.

- **Clean Energy Transmission and Reliability ($32.0 million)**
  The Clean Energy Transmission and Reliability (CETR) Program enhances the reliability of interdependent energy systems by developing advanced transmission-driven technologies that improve grid reliability, efficiency, and security; and advanced modeling capabilities to improve electric system planning and operations. The FY 2014 Budget Request includes a new subprogram, Energy Systems Predictive Capability, to highlight efforts to develop simulations and predictive analytic tools that provide real time situational awareness responses to energy supply disruptions, such as electricity and fuel outages.

- **Smart Grid ($14.4 million)**
  The Smart Grid Program targets modernization of the electric system at the distribution level, with the goals of self-healing from grid disturbances for improved reliability system efficiency. In FY 2014, the program focus includes advanced communications and controls, microgrid development, and Smart Grid standards and protocols for increased interoperability.

- **Electricity Systems Hub ($20.0 million)**
  The FY 2014 Budget Request establishes the Electricity Systems Hub to address fundamental science, technology, economic, and policy issues that affect our ability to achieve a seamless and modernized grid.

- **Cybersecurity for Energy Delivery System ($38.0 million)**
  The Cybersecurity for Energy Delivery System (CEDS) program develops advanced cybersecurity technologies and capabilities to reduce the risk of energy disruptions due to cyber events. The FY 2014 Budget Request increases efforts to enhance situational awareness and strengthen operational capabilities to help the energy sector cost effectively manage cybersecurity risks to increase the resiliency of the energy systems.

- **Energy Storage ($15.0 million)**
  The Energy Storage program works to accelerate the development of affordable advanced grid-scale energy storage to enhance the stability, reliability, and flexibility of the electric grid. In FY 2014, as one type of rechargeable flow battery transitions to industry, the program focuses on developing nitrogen-oxygen batteries and demonstrating a prototype of medium-temperature, planar sodium battery.

- **National Electricity Delivery ($6.0 million)**
  National Electricity Delivery (NED), previously called the Permitting, Siting, and Analysis program, provides technical assistance to states and regions to help facilitate the development of reliable and affordable electricity infrastructure; and authorizes electricity exports and permits cross-border transmission infrastructure under the Federal Power Act. In FY 2014, NED streamlines siting of transmission facilities on Federal lands by leading the development of a pre-application process to encourage early coordination between Federal agencies and potential applicants.

- **Infrastructure Security and Energy Restoration ($16.0 million)**
  The Infrastructure Security and Energy Restoration (ISER) program leads efforts to help secure the U.S. energy infrastructure against hazards, reducing the impact of disruptive events, and responding to and facilitating recovery from energy disruptions in collaboration with industry, States and local governments. The FY 2014 Budget Request includes a new Operational Energy and Resilience initiative to enhance the Department's emergency response capabilities, including building a state-of-the-art Energy Resilience and Operations Center, and placing Federal energy experts in the field to implement resiliency solutions and improve response time during emergencies.

- **Program Direction ($27.6 million)**
  Program Direction funds federal staff and support services for the management, oversight, and technical direction of OE.

		(discretionary dollars in thousands)			
	FY 2012 Current	FY 2013 Annualized CR	FY 2014 Request	FY 2014 vs. FY 2012	
				$	%
Fossil Energy Research and Development	524,074	536,969	429,275	-94,799	-18.1%
Naval Petroleum & Oil Shale Reserves	14,909	15,000	20,000	+5,091	+34.1%
Strategic Petroleum Reserve	192,704	193,883	189,400	-3,304	-1.7%
Northeast Home Heating Oil Reserve	10,119	10,181	8,000	-2,119	-20.9%
Adjustments	-187,000	-42,000	-8,700	+178,300	+95.3%
Total, Fossil Energy	**554,806**	**714,033**	**637,975**	**+83,169**	**+15.0%**
Coal	359,320	370,650	276,631	-82,689	-23.0%
Natural Gas Technologies	14,575	15,083	17,000	+2,425	+16.6%
Unconventional Fossil Energy Technologies	4,859	5,027	0	-4,859	-100.0%
Program Direction	119,929	120,663	115,753	-4,176	-3.5%
Plant and Capital Equipment	16,794	16,897	13,294	-3,500	-20.8%
Fossil Energy Environmental Restoration	7,897	7,945	5,897	-2,000	-25.3%
Special Recruitment Programs	700	704	700	0	N/A
Subtotal, Fossil Energy Research and Development	*524,074*	*536,969*	*429,275*	*-94,799*	*-18.1%*
Adjustments	-187,000	-42,000	-8,700	+178,300	+95.3%
Total, Fossil Energy Research And Development	**337,074**	**494,969**	**420,575**	**+83,501**	**+24.8%**
Facilities Development and Operations	170,914	171,960	164,741	-6,173	-3.6%
Management for SPR Operations	21,790	21,923	24,659	+2,869	+13.2%
Total, Strategic Petroleum Reserve	**192,704**	**193,883**	**189,400**	**-3,304**	**-1.7%**
Northeast Home Heating Oil Reserve	10,119	10,181	8,000	-2,119	-20.9%
Total, Northeast Home Heating Oil Reserve	**10,119**	**10,181**	**8,000**	**-2,119**	**-20.9%**
Production Operations	5,480	5,513	13,000	+7,520	+137.2%
Management	9,429	9,487	7,000	-2,429	-25.8%
Total, Naval Petroleum & Oil Shale Reserves	**14,909**	**15,000**	**20,000**	**5,091**	**+34.1%**

The **Office of Fossil Energy (FE)** FY 2014 Budget Request manages multiple programs which are described below.

Fossil Energy Research and Development ($420.3 million)
The Fossil Energy Research and Development (FER&D) program advances technologies related to the reliable, efficient, affordable, and environmentally sound use of fossil fuels which are essential to our Nation's security and economic prosperity. FE leads Federal research, development, and demonstration efforts on advanced carbon capture, and storage (CCS) technologies to facilitate achievement of the President's climate goals. FE also develops technological solutions for the prudent and sustainable development of our unconventional domestic resources.

- **Carbon Capture & Storage and Power Systems ($276.6 million)**
  The Carbon Capture and Storage (CCS) and Power Systems program conducts research to reduce carbon emissions by improving the performance and efficiency of fossil energy systems and CCS technologies.

  - **Carbon Capture ($112 million)**
    The Carbon Capture activity is focused on the development of post-combustion and pre-combustion CO_2 capture and compression technologies for new and existing power plants. Post-combustion CO2 capture technology R&D is focused on pulverized coal (PC) power plants, which is the current standard industry technology for coal-fueled electricity generation. The Natural Gas Capture subactivity is focused on facilitating the demonstration of the first commercial natural gas combined cycle (NGCC)

power plant to capture and store 75% or more of the CO_2 emissions. Pre-combustion CO_2 capture is applicable to gasification-based systems such as Integrated Gasification Combine Cycle (IGCC), a potential technology for future generation of electricity from coal-fueled plants.

- o **Carbon Storage ($61.1 million)**
  The overall goal of the Carbon Storage Program is to develop and validate technologies to ensure safe and permanent geologic storage of captured CO_2. Development and validation of these technologies is critical to ensure industry and regulatory agencies have the capability to monitor and account for CO_2 and ensure the viability of carbon storage as an effective technology solution that can be implemented on a large-scale to mitigate carbon emissions.

- o **Advanced Energy Systems ($48 million)**
  The Advanced Energy Systems (AES) mission is to increase the availability and efficiency of fossil energy systems integrated with CO_2 capture, while maintaining the highest environmental standards. The program elements focus on gasification, oxy-combustion, advanced turbines, and other energy systems. While the primary focus is on coal-based power systems, improvements to many of these technologies will result in positive spillover benefits that also reduce the cost of converting other carbon-based materials, such as biomass, petcoke or natural gas, into power and value-added products in an environmentally-acceptable manner.

- o **Cross-cutting Research ($20.5 million)**
  The Cross-cutting Research activity serves as a bridge between basic and applied research by fostering the development of innovative systems for improving availability, efficiency, and environmental performance of fossil energy systems with carbon capture and storage. This crosscutting effort is implemented through the research and development of sensors, controls, and advanced materials. This program area also develops computation, simulation, and modeling tools focused on optimizing plant design and shortening developmental timelines.

- o **NETL Coal Research and Development ($35.0 million)**
  This activity supports Federal researchers who conduct basic and applied research activities in Carbon Capture, Carbon Storage, Advanced Energy Systems, and Cross Cutting Research.

- **Natural Gas Technologies ($17.0 million)**
  The Natural Gas Technologies program supports a collaborative research and development initiative with the Environmental Protection Agency (EPA) and the Department of the Interior's U.S. Geological Survey (USGS) to understand and minimize the potential environmental, health, and safety impacts of natural gas development through hydraulic fracturing (fracking). The program also conducts research designed to further our understanding of the occurrence, nature, and behavior of naturally-occurring gas hydrates and the resulting resource, hazard, and environmental implications.

  [Other FER&D Program elements are Program Direction, Plant & Capital Equipment, Environmental Restoration, and Special Recruitment programs which make up the total budget]

Strategic Petroleum Reserve ($189.4 million)
The Strategic Petroleum Reserve (SPR) provides strategic and economic security against foreign and domestic disruptions in oil supplies via an emergency stockpile of crude oil. The program fulfills U.S. obligations under the International Energy Program, which avails the U.S. of International Energy Agency assistance through its coordinated energy emergency response plans, and provides a deterrent against energy supply disruptions. The FY 2014 Budget Request provides for the management, maintenance, security and operational readiness of the SPR's oil storage and distribution facilities.

Northeast Home Heating Oil Reserve ($8.0 million)

The Northeast Home Heating Oil Reserve (NEHHOR) continues to maintain a 1 million barrel inventory of ultra-low sulfur distillate, stored in the Northeast commercial storage terminals, to provide a short-term supplement to the Northeast systems' commercial supply of heating oil for deployment in the event of an emergency supply disruption.

Naval Petroleum and Oil Shale Reserve ($20.0 million)

Naval Petroleum and Oil Shale Reserve (NPOSR) will continue to work on environmental remediation at NPR-1 and will continue disposition activities, including environmental remediation, at NPR-3. Production facilities at NPR-3 will remain operational as long as economic. The program will continue Rocky Mountain Oilfield Testing Center (RMOTC) testing for 100% funds-in projects. Environmental remediation of NPR-3 facilities will continue to facilitate the sale/disposition of the property in a manner consistent with an approved property sale/disposition plan. Final disposition of the property is estimated to occur in FY 2015.

	FY 2012 Current	FY 2013 Annualized CR	FY 2014 Request	FY 2014 vs. FY 2012 (discretionary dollars in thousands)	
				$	%
Nuclear Energy Enabling Technologies	71,307	75,127	62,300	-9,007	-12.6%
Integrated University Program	5,000	5,031	0	-5,000	-100.0%
Small Modular Reactor Licensing Technical Support	67,000	67,410	70,000	+3,000	+4.5%
Reactor Concepts RD&D	110,652	115,574	72,500	-38,152	-34.5%
Fuel Cycle R&D	180,993	187,400	165,100	-15,893	-8.8%
International Nuclear Energy Cooperation	2,983	3,001	2,500	-483	-16.2%
Radiological Facilities Management	69,510	69,935	5,000	-64,510	-92.8%
Idaho Facilities Management	154,097	155,040	181,560	+27,463	+17.8%
Idaho Sitewide Safeguards and Security	0	0	94,000	+94,000	N/A
Program Direction	91,000	91,557	87,500	-3,500	-3.8%
Subtotal, Nuclear Energy	*752,542*	*770,075*	*740,460*	*-12,082*	*-1.6%*
Adjustments	7,924	0	-5,000	-12,924	-163.1%
Subtotal, Nuclear Energy	*760,466*	*770,075*	*735,460*	*-25,006*	*-3.3%*
Other Defense Activities					
Idaho Sitewide Safeguards and Security	93,350	93,921	0	-93,350	-100.0%
Total, Nuclear Energy	**853,816**	**863,996**	**735,460**	**-118,356**	**-13.9%**

*Note: Includes the planned use of unobligated balances.

The **Office of Nuclear Energy (NE)** supports the diverse civilian nuclear energy programs of the U.S. Government, leading Federal efforts to research and develop nuclear energy technologies, including generation, safety, waste storage and management, and security technologies, to help meet energy security, proliferation resistance, and climate goals.

- **Small Modular Reactor Licensing Technical Support ($70.0 million)**
  The Small Modular Reactor (SMR) Licensing Technical Support (LTS) program accelerates the timelines for the commercialization and deployment of small modular reactor technologies. The mission of the program is to support first-of-a-kind costs associated with design certification and licensing activities for SMR designs through cost-shared arrangements with industry partners (industry contributions are a minimum of 50% of the cost) to promote the deployment of SMRs that can provide safe, clean, affordable power. If industry chooses to widely deploy these technologies in the U.S., they could help meet the nation's economic, energy security and climate change goals. DOE will have all awarded cooperative agreements in place by FY 2014.

- **Reactor Concepts Research, Development and Demonstration ($72.5 million)**
  The Reactor Concepts Research, Development and Demonstration (RCRD&D) program is designed to advance the state of reactor technology to improve its competitiveness, and help advance nuclear power as a resource capable of meeting the Nation's energy, environmental, and national security needs. RD&D activities are designed to address technical, cost, safety and security issues associated with reactor concepts including advanced Small Modular Reactors (SMRs) and other advanced reactor concepts. In FY 2014 RCRD&D is shifting focus away from the development and demonstration of the Next Generation Nuclear Plant toward longer term research on Advanced Reactor Concepts.

- **Fuel Cycle Research and Development ($165.1 million)**
  In FY 2014 the Fuel Cycle Research and Development (FCR&D) program supports the *Strategy for the Management and Disposal of Used Nuclear Fuel and High-Level Waste* by funding activities to lay the ground work for the design of an integrated waste management system as well as related research and development work. The FCR&D program will also conduct R&D a suite of technology options that will enable future decision makers to make informed decisions about how better to manage nuclear waste and

used fuel from reactors. The program employs a long-term, science-based approach to foster innovative, transformational technology solutions to achieve this mission.

- **Nuclear Energy Enabling Technologies ($62.3 million)**
  The Nuclear Energy Enabling Technologies (NEET) program is designed to conduct research and development in crosscutting technologies that directly support the development of new and advanced reactor designs and fuel cycle technologies, as well as the potential extension of life of the current fleet of nuclear reactors. These technologies are expected to help advance the state of nuclear technology, improving its competitiveness, and promoting continued contribution to meeting our Nation's energy and environmental challenges.

- **Radiological Facilities Management ($5.0 million)**
  The Office of Nuclear Energy provides radioisotope power systems for non-NE and non-DOE space missions. These activities have been split funded by NE, through the Radiological Facilities Management program, and by the user agencies, primarily the National Aeronautics and Space Administration. Starting in FY 2014, these activities are transitioning to a full cost recovery funding model and are included in the National Aeronautics and Space Administration budget request. Radiological Facilities Management's Research Reactor Infrastructure program continues to provide fresh reactor fuel to, and removes used fuel from, 26 operating university reactors.

- **Idaho Facilities Management and Idaho Sitewide Safeguards and Security ($275.6 million)**
  The mission of the Idaho Facilities Management (IFM) and Idaho Sitewide Safeguards and Security (S&S) programs are to manage the planning, acquisition, operation, maintenance, security, and disposition of the NE-owned facilities and capabilities at the Idaho National Laboratory (INL). The IFM and S&S programs maintain DOE mission-supporting facilities and capabilities at INL in a secure, safe, compliant status to support the Department's nuclear energy research, testing of naval reactor fuels and reactor core components, and range of national security technology programs that support the National Nuclear Security Administration (NNSA) and other Federal agencies such as the Department of Homeland Security in the areas of critical infrastructure protection and nuclear nonproliferation. FY 2014 activities include the continuation of work to resume transient testing capabilities and continued funding for the Remote-Handled Low Level Waste Disposal Project.

Race to the Top for Energy Efficiency and Grid Modernization

	FY 2012 Current	FY 2013 Annualized CR	FY 2014 Request	FY 2014 vs. FY 2012 (discretionary dollars in thousands)	
				$	%
Race to the Top for Energy Efficiency and Grid Modernization	0	0	200,000	+200,000	N/A
Total, Race to the Top for Energy Efficiency and Grid Modernization	0	0	200,000	+200,000	N/A

Race to the Top for Energy Efficiency and Grid Modernization ($200 million)

Challenges States to Cut Energy Waste, Support Energy Efficiency, and Modernize the Grid: the FY 2014 Budget Request includes one-time funding for a new Race to the Top that challenges States, tribes, local governments with public power authorities, and co-operatives to implement effective policies to cut energy waste and modernize the grid.

Key opportunities for states and other eligible applicants include: modernizing utility regulations and adopting policies to encourage cost-effective investments in efficiency, including combined heat and power and demand response resources; clean distributed generation; enhancing customer access to data; investments that improve the reliability, security and resilience of the grid; and enhancing the sharing of information regarding grid conditions.

This initiative supports the President's goal of doubling energy productivity above 2010 levels by 2030.

	FY 2012 Current	FY 2013 Annualized CR*	FY 2014 Request	FY 2014 vs. FY 2012 (discretionary dollars in thousands)	
				$	%
Carlsbad	213,334	---	203,390	-9,944	-4.7%
Idaho	389,800	---	370,010	-19,790	-5.1%
Oak Ridge	399,265	---	394,017	-5,248	-1.3%
Paducah	133,647	---	312,090	+178,443	+133.5%
Portsmouth	238,115	---	142,965	-95,150	-40.0%
Richland	952,746	---	924,330	-28,416	-3.0%
River Protection	1,182,010	---	1,210,216	+28,206	+2.4%
Savannah River	1,187,782	---	1,088,261	-99,521	-8.4%
Lawrence Livermore National Laboratory	2,173	---	1,476	-697	-32.1%
Los Alamos National Laboratory	188,161	---	219,789	+31,628	+16.8%
Nevada	65,145	---	61,897	-3,248	-5.0%
Sandia National Laboratories	2,814	---	2,814	0	N/A
Separation Process Research Unit	23,700	---	23,700	0	N/A
West Valley demonstration project	64,735	---	64,000	-735	-1.1%
Brookhaven National Laboratory	12,535	---	0	-12,535	-100.0%
Energy Technology Engineering Center	6,279	---	9,411	+3,132	+49.9%
Moab	30,625	---	35,778	+5,153	+16.8%
SLAC National Accelerator Laboratory	2,935	---	0	-2,935	-100.0%
All Other Sites	14,703	---	4,702	-10,001	-68.0%
Headquarters Operations	30,689	---	37,979	+7,290	+23.8%
Program Direction	321,628	---	280,784	-40,844	-12.7%
Safeguards and Security	250,968	---	234,079	-16,889	-6.7%
Federal Contribution to Uranium Enrichment Decontamination and	0	---	463,000	+463,000	N/A
Subtotal, Environmental Management by Site	*5,713,789*	*5,748,786*	*6,084,688*	*+370,899*	*+6.5%*
Use of Prior Year Balances	-3,381	-3,402	0	+3,381	+100.0%
UED&D Fund Discretionary Payment	0	0	-463,000	-463,000	N/A
Total, Environmental Management by Site	**5,710,408**	**5,745,384**	**5,621,688**	**-88,720**	**-1.6%**

Note: FY 2013 amounts shown reflect the P.L. 112 175 continuing resolution level annualized to a full year. These amounts are shown only at the "congressional control" level and above; below that level a dash (---) is shown.

The **Environmental Management** program will support the Department's Strategic Plan to complete the environmental remediation of legacy and active sites, while protecting human health and the environment. The program has two goals: Reduce the Department's Cold War legacy environmental footprint and to develop novel methods to accelerate progress and reduce costs.

The following are key elements and efforts around the EM complex:

- **Carlsbad ($203.4 million)**
  The Carlsbad Field Office has the responsibility for management of the National Transuranic Waste Program and the Waste Isolation Pilot Plant, the Nation's only mined geologic repository for the permanent disposal of defense-generated transuranic waste. The Carlsbad Field Office's National Transuranic Waste Program coordinates with all DOE sites that generate transuranic waste to retrieve, repackage, characterize, ship, and dispose of transuranic waste resulting in cleaning up sites, reducing risks, and decreasing nuclear footprints. This involves a number of activities: characterizing, transporting, storing and disposing of legacy transuranic wastes that have been stored at DOE sites for decades, as well as, transuranic wastes generated through ongoing facility deactivation, environmental remediation activities at currently contaminated DOE sites and transuranic wastes generated by other DOE mission activities.

- **Paducah ($312.1 million)**

  The Paducah site supports maintaining the depleted uranium hexafluoride (DUF6) Conversion Facility operations at full capacity, continued landfill operations, pump and treat operations, and remediation of groundwater. Site planning includes the mid-year transition of the gaseous diffusion plant facilities (in a cold and dry state) from the United States Enrichment Corporation to the Department of Energy. The Paducah site's overall environmental cleanup strategy is based on taking near-term actions to control or eliminate ongoing sources of contamination along with continued investigation of other potential sources.

- **Hanford Site (Richland) ($924.3 million)**

  The Richland Operations Office manages the Hanford site cleanup activities associated with the production of nuclear materials during the Cold War, including soil and groundwater remediation, facility decontamination and decommissioning (D&D), stabilization and disposition of nuclear materials and spent nuclear fuel, and disposition of waste other than high-level waste, which is managed by the Office of River Protection.

  The strategy of the Richland site is to shrink the active footprint of cleanup from 586 square miles to less than 75 square miles by completing the majority of the cleanup of the Hanford's Columbia River Corridor by 2015. The next focus is on cleanup of the Central Plateau which includes demolishing the Plutonium Finishing Plant by 2016, and deactivating and demolishing over 80 facilities/structures; eliminating the highest risk nuclear facility on the Hanford Site.

- **Office of River Protection ($1,210.2 million)**

  The Office of River Protection's primary goal is the safe management and treatment of approximately 56 million gallons of high-level radioactive liquid waste in 177 underground storage tanks at Hanford. The Office of River Protection is responsible for the storage, retrieval, treatment, immobilization, and disposal of liquid tank waste and operation, maintenance, engineering, and construction activities in the Tank Farms. A multi-year construction project to build a Waste Treatment and Immobilization Plant to process and immobilize the tank waste is ongoing.

  The end state is to clean up the tank waste and tank farms in a compliant manner; immobilize and facilitate safe disposal of associated radioactive and chemical wastes; and protect human health, the environment, and Columbia River resources. The Office of River Protection's cleanup strategy is a risk-based approach that focuses on contamination sources that are the greatest contributors to risk.

- **Savannah River ($1,088.2 million)**

  At the Savannah River Site, the largest portion of the request supports the Tank Waste Liquid Waste Management Program, which includes the operation of the Defense Waste Processing Facility, as well as, operation of the Actinide Removal Process and Modular Caustic Side Extraction units. These units will be needed through construction of the Salt Waste Processing Facility. This request also supports the operation of the Saltstone Facility and the continued closure activities for Tanks 5 and 6.

  The site will also continue to support the management of Special Nuclear Materials including the processing of vulnerable spent nuclear fuel; the Global Threat Reduction initiative through continued receipt of foreign and domestic research reactor spent (used) nuclear fuel; and activities to expand the storage capacity and extend the life of L-Basin. This request also supports continued activities to reduce the residual plutonium contamination in Building 235-F consistent with Defense Nuclear Safety Facilities Board Recommendation 2012-1.

  The Savannah River site will work aggressively to reduce its footprint. To accomplish this goal the site will stabilize, treat, and/or disposition a variety of radioactive and hazardous waste streams; will remediate contaminated soil and groundwater; will deactivate and decommission excess facilities; and will dispose of the inventory of nuclear materials, spent (used) nuclear fuel, and high level waste.

	(discretionary dollars in thousands)				
	FY 2012 Current	FY 2013 Annualized CR	FY 2014 Request	FY 2014 vs. FY 2012	
				$	%
Legacy Management	157,514	158,478	163,271	+5,757	+3.7%
Program Direction	12,086	12,160	13,712	+1,626	+13.5%
Total, Legacy Management	**169,600**	**170,638**	**176,983**	**+7,383**	**+4.4%**

The **Office of Legacy Management (LM)** ensures the sustainable protection of human health and the environment after site cleanup is completed. LM's responsibilities include DOE closure sites, former uranium mills, sites in the Formerly Utilized Remedial Action Program, and selected sites conveyed to DOE under other authority. LM also funds the pensions and post-retirement benefits for former contractor personnel after site closure. The majority of LM's activities are long term and focus on maintaining the Department's legal, regulatory, and contractual commitments. Management of closure site activities by LM enables other DOE programs to concentrate on risk reduction and site closure. By the end of FY 2014, LM expects to have responsibility for long-term management of almost 100 sites.

LM's functions span both physical and human resources. In the physical environment, LM conducts long-term surveillance and maintenance of environmental remedies (e.g., groundwater monitoring and disposal cell maintenance) to protect human health and the environment. For each of the sites LM maintains both the physical and electronic records and responds to over 1,000 requests for information each year. LM is also responsible for maintaining the records and information systems for the Yucca Mountain site, including the Licensing Support Network. LM funds the pension plan contributions and post-retirement benefits (e.g., medical and life insurance) for former contractor workers from eight sites. In addition, LM manages the sites' natural resources, promotes reuse, is responsible for the Department's uranium leasing program and, where possible, transfers sites to external parties.

The LM program supports the Department's Goal of Keeping Americans Safe by Environmental Efforts through its actions to protect the public from harmful exposure to radioactive waste and nuclear materials at remediated sites. LM is also a leader in cutting resource waste, supporting energy efficiency and reducing energy use in Federal buildings, including certification by the U.S. Green Building Council for the LM records storage facility. LM has submitted a proposal to the Office of Management and Budget for redesignation as a High Performing Organization – a designation it has held since 2007.

	FY 2012 Current	FY 2013 Annualized CR	FY 2014 Request	FY 2014 vs. FY 2012 (discretionary dollars in thousands)	
				$	%
Advanced Research Projects Agency - Energy Projects	253,000	256,561	344,890	+91,890	+36.3%
Program Direction	22,000	20,122	34,110	+12,110	+55.0%
Total, Advanced Research Projects Agency - Energy	**275,000**	**276,683**	**379,000**	**+104,000**	**+37.8%**

The **Advanced Research Projects Agency – Energy (ARPA-E)** mission is to support early-stage energy technology innovations that will enhance the economic and energy security of the United States through the development of transformational technologies that reduce America's dependence on foreign energy imports; reduce U.S. energy related emissions, including greenhouse gases; improve energy efficiency across all sectors of the U.S. economy; and ensure the U.S. maintains a technological lead in the development and deployment of advanced energy technologies. ARPA-E achieves this mission by identifying and promoting advances in fundamental and applied sciences; translating scientific discoveries and cutting-edge inventions into technological innovations; and accelerating transformational technological advances in areas that industry by itself is not likely to undertake because of technical and financial uncertainty.

ARPA-E demands a credible path to commercialization when launching projects and has a dedicated technology-to-market team to assist its performers. ARPA-E performers have experienced several notable technological successes and formed strong partnerships in both the public and private sector, including: doubling the world record energy density for a rechargeable lithium-ion battery (to 400 Whr/kg); developing a 1 megawatt silicon carbide transistor the size of a fingernail; engineering microbes that use hydrogen and carbon dioxide to make liquid transportation fuel; pioneering a near-isothermal compressed air energy storage system; partnering with the U.S. Navy to advance research on heating and air conditioning efficiency; launching new companies in grid scale batteries, biofuels, and efficient thermo devices; and garnering over $450 million in follow-on private-sector funding.

ARPA-E selects potential investment areas by considering the science and technology landscape, the market landscape, and the regulatory landscape. ARPA-E will invest only in instances where circumstances in these areas are aligned to enable transformative, breakthrough discoveries that have the potential to be brought to market scale. The FY 2014 Budget Request supports the President's goals of accelerating transformation of America's energy system, securing U.S. leadership in clean energy technology and investing in science and innovation as the cornerstone of our nation's economic prosperity. ARPA-E has two broad thematic strategic thrusts: Transportation Systems and Stationary Power Systems.

- **Transportation Systems ($197.0 million)**
  The ARPA-E Transportation Systems thrust seeks to create a diverse portfolio of technological options that would reduce our dependence on oil while also focusing on reducing fuel consumption and energy-related emissions.

- **Stationary Power Systems ($148.0 million)**
  ARPA-E's efforts in the Stationary Power Systems thrust seek to create a diverse array of technological options that would reduce energy demand and greenhouse gas emissions, create low-cost power generation from renewable sources, provide greater reliability and security in the delivery of electricity, and provide a secure energy foundation for the future.

	FY 2012 Current	FY 2013 Annualized CR	FY 2014 Request	FY 2014 vs. FY 2012 (discretionary dollars in thousands)	
				$	%
Advanced Scientific Computing Research	428,304	443,566	465,593	+37,289	+8.7%
Basic Energy Sciences	1,644,767	1,698,424	1,862,411	+217,644	+13.2%
Biological and Environmental Research	592,433	613,287	625,347	+32,914	+5.6%
Fusion Energy Sciences Program	392,957	403,450	458,324	+65,367	+16.6%
High Energy Physics	770,533	795,701	776,521	+5,988	+0.8%
Nuclear Physics	534,642	550,737	569,938	+35,296	+6.6%
Workforce Development for Teachers and Scientist	18,500	18,613	16,500	-2,000	-10.8%
Science Laboratories Infrastructure	111,800	112,485	97,818	-13,982	-12.5%
Safeguards and Security	80,573	81,066	87,000	+6,427	+8.0%
Science Program Direction	185,000	186,132	193,300	+8,300	+4.5%
Small Business Innovation Research (SBIR)	175,471	0	0	-175,471	-100.0%
Total, Science	**4,934,980**	**4,903,461**	**5,152,752**	**+217,772**	**+4.4%**

Office of Science (SC) programs contribute to the achievement of all DOE Strategic Plan goals and the investment in clean energy, innovation, and the future jobs theme of the FY 2014 Budget Request. SC is the largest federal sponsor of basic research in the physical sciences and supports programs in areas such as physics, chemistry, biology, environmental science, applied mathematics, and computational science. SC supports investigators at about 300 academic institutions and all of the DOE laboratories. Approximately 29,000 researchers from universities, national laboratories, industry, and international partners are expected to use SC facilities in FY 2014. Highlights for the SC research programs follow:

- **Advanced Scientific Computing Research ($465.6 million)**
  Advanced Scientific Computing Research (ASCR) advances applied mathematics and computer science; delivers, in partnership with disciplinary science programs, advanced computational scientific applications; enhances computing and networking capabilities; and develops, in partnership with U.S. industry, future generations of computing hardware and tools for science. The FY 2014 Budget Request addresses technical challenges to delivering 1,000 fold increases in computing capability. Increased funding will support operations, lease payments, and user support for ASCR facilities.

- **Basic Energy Sciences ($1,862.4 million)**
  Basic Energy Sciences (BES) supports fundamental research to understand, predict, and control matter and energy to provide the foundation for new energy technologies and to mitigate the environmental impacts of energy use. In FY 2014, BES will support ongoing core research, Energy Frontier Research Centers (EFRCs), and the Fuels from Sunlight and the Batteries and Energy Storage Energy Innovation Hubs. The EFRCs will undergo an open re-competition that will include selection of new EFRCs and consider renewal applications for existing EFRCs. In FY 2014, BES will support the National Synchrotron Light Source-II construction and early operations, Linac Coherent Light Source-II construction, the operations of the five synchrotron light source facilities, five Nanoscale Science Research Centers, and the three neutron scattering facilities. Major item of equipment projects for the Advanced Photon Source Upgrade and the National Synchrotron Light Source –II (NSLS-II) Experimental Tools continue.

- **Biological and Environmental Research ($625.3 million)**
  Biological and Environmental Research (BER) supports the Department's energy and environmental missions. Its research includes efforts to understand how genomic information is translated to functional capabilities, enabling more confident redesign of microbes and plants for sustainable biofuels production, improved carbon storage, and contaminant bioremediation. BER research advances our understanding of the role of atmospheric, terrestrial, ocean, and subsurface interactions in determining climate dynamics to

predict future climate change and plan for future energy and resource needs. In FY 2014, support of research and scientific user facilities in bioenergy, climate, and environmental science continues. Increased investments target the development of biosystems design tools and the development of integrative analysis of experimental datasets in support of bioenergy, climate, and environmental research. Research in foundational genomics, including the DOE Bioenergy Research Centers, will provide the fundamental biological system science to underpin advances in clean energy through bioenergy production and carbon cycling. Climate and Environmental Research activities will explore interaction between geography, clouds, aerosols, and sensitive ecosystems and the sensitivity and uncertainty of climate predictions and models.

- **Fusion Energy Sciences ($458.3 million)**
Fusion Energy Sciences (FES) supports research to develop fusion as a future energy source. The FY 2014 Budget Request funds U.S. contributions to the ITER project for long-lead procurements required in construction of the facility; the majority of these contributions will be spent on in-kind hardware sourced from U.S. industries, national laboratories, and universities. Domestic research continues in most areas, while program balance is maintained consistent with National Academies recommendations to promote overall federal stewardship of plasma science.

- **High Energy Physics ($776.5 million)**
High Energy Physics (HEP) supports research to understand how the universe works at its most fundamental level. Support for Large Hadron Collider (LHC) detector operations, maintenance, computing, and R&D for detector upgrades continue. Project engineering and design for the Muon to Electron Conversion Experiment (Mu2e) continues as well as research for the Long Baseline Neutrino Experiment. Exploration of the feasibility of neutrino and dark matter research continues. Collaborations on projects to pursue questions in dark matter, dark energy, and neutrino properties are pursued. Support for collaborative advanced accelerator and detector R&D including development of superconducting radio frequency technology applicable to accelerator projects continues as well. The FY 2014 Budget supports new accelerator science stewardship activities that can broadly benefit fields both within and outside of HEP.

- **Nuclear Physics ($569.9 million)**
Nuclear Physics (NP) supports research to discover, explore, and understand all forms of nuclear matter. The FY 2014 Budget Request supports construction of the Facility for Rare Isotope Beam (FRIB) at Michigan State University to provide world-leading capability and new discovery potential for U.S. leadership in nuclear structure and nuclear astrophysics, and continued U.S. scientific competency in critical areas. The Relativistic Heavy Ion Collider (RHIC) and the Argonne Tandem Linac Accelerator System (ATLAS) are supported for world leading research on new states of matter and the origin of heavy nuclei. Construction continues for the 12 GeV Continuous Electron Beam Accelerator Facility (CEBAF) Upgrade, and beam development and commissioning activities are initiated.

	FY 2012 Current	FY 2013 Annualized CR	FY 2014 Request	FY 2014 vs. FY 2012 (discretionary dollars in thousands)	
				$	%
Administrative Operations:					
Office of the Secretary	5,030	5,061	5,008	-22	-0.4%
Chief Financial Officer	53,204	53,530	51,204	-2,000	-3.8%
Chief Information Officer	84,628	86,454	79,857	-4,771	-5.6%
Congressional & Intergovernmental Affairs	4,690	4,719	4,700	+10	+0.2%
Economic Impact and Diversity	7,473	7,519	9,806	+2,333	+31.2%
General Counsel	33,053	33,255	33,053	0	N/A
Human Capital	25,089	23,230	24,488	-601	-2.4%
Indian Energy Policy and Programs	2,000	2,012	2,506	+506	+25.3%
Management	61,993	63,077	55,699	-6,294	-10.2%
Policy and International Affairs	26,961	27,126	26,961	0	N/A
Public Affairs	3,801	3,824	3,597	-204	-5.4%
Funding from Other Defense Activities	-118,836	-119,563	-118,836	0	N/A
Subtotal, Administrative Operations	*189,086*	*190,244*	*178,043*	*-11,043*	*-5.8%*
Cost of Work for Others	48,537	48,834	48,537	0	N/A
Miscellaneous Revenues	-111,623	-112,306	-108,188	+3,435	+3.1%
Subtotal, Cost of Work/Revenues	*-63,086*	*-63,472*	*-59,651*	*+3,435*	*+5.4%*
Total, Departmental Administration	**126,000**	**126,772**	**118,392**	**-7,608**	**-6.0%**

The **Departmental Administration (DA)** appropriation funds 11 DOE-wide management organizations under Administrative Operations. These organizations support headquarters operations in human resources, administration, accounting, budgeting, program analysis, project management, information management, legal services, life-cycle asset management, workforce diversity, Indian energy policy, minority economic impact, policy, international affairs, congressional and intergovernmental liaison, and public affairs. Funding for the Office of the Secretary is provided separately from the other administrative functions within the DA appropriation. The DA appropriation also budgets for **Cost of Work for Others** and receives Miscellaneous Revenues from other sources. The Department has established 52 Measures of Performance to assure Management and Operational effectiveness and efficiencies in safe and secure mission execution. Collectively these are cross cutting and complex business elements that support the business operations and allow internal and external senior leaders to drive improvements in decision making, operations, authorities, communication, and ensure costs are aligned with strategic outputs.

In FY 2014, additional funding has been set aside to support the **Office of Economic Impact and Diversity**. The budget increase will primarily support an expansion of outreach initiatives by the Office of Small and Disadvantaged Business Utilization to better engage small businesses in contracting opportunities at the Department.

Funding for the **Office of Indian Energy Policy and Programs** maintains initiatives developed in FY 2011 and implemented in FY 2012, and it covers the increase in support costs for energy development and generation.

Funding level supports an increase in **Cybersecurity** activities within the **Office of the Chief Information Officer** to support enhancement of critical incident management programs.

DOE also operates a Working Capital Fund (WCF) as a financial tool to improve management of common administration services. The objectives of the WCF are to fairly allocate costs to mission programs; to offer better choices on amount, quality, and sources of services; and to provide flexibility for service providers to respond to customer needs.

Hearings and Appeals

| | (discretionary dollars in thousands) | | | | |
| | FY 2012 Current | FY 2013 Annualized CR | FY 2014 Request | FY 2014 vs. FY 2012 | |
				$	%
Hearings And Appeals	4,142	4,167	5,022	+880	+21.2%
Total, Hearings and Appeals	**4,142**	**4,167**	**5,022**	**+880**	**+21.2%**

The **Office of Hearings and Appeals (OHA)** is responsible for all DOE adjudicative processes except those administered by the Federal Energy Regulatory Commission. OHA's jurisdiction includes Freedom of Information Act and Privacy Act appeals, evidentiary hearings to determine an employee's eligibility for a security clearance, appeals and agency decisions on contractor employee whistleblower complaints, and requests for exception from DOE regulations and orders, such as exceptions from the appliance efficiency regulations. In 2012, the alternative dispute resolution function was transferred from the Office of the General Counsel to OHA. The FY 2014 Budget request reflects an increase due to this function transfer and related 4 FTEs.

The Request supports salaries and benefits for 24 FTEs, including 4 FTEs associated with the Alternative Dispute Resolution function.

Advanced Technology Vehicles Manufacturing Loan Program

				(discretionary dollars in thousands)	
	FY 2012 Current	FY 2013 Annualized CR	FY 2014 Request	FY 2014 vs. FY 2012	
				$	%
Advanced Technology Vehicles Manufacturing Loan Program	6,000	6,037	6,000	0	N/A
Total, Advanced Technology Vehicles Manufacturing Loan Program	**6,000**	**6,037**	**6,000**	**0**	**N/A**

The **Advanced Technologies Vehicles Manufacturing (ATVM) Loan Program** supports the development of advanced technology vehicles and associated components in the United States. The ATVM Loan Program has closed over $8 billion in loans for five projects. These projects are projected to fund over 30,000 jobs in the United States and save approximately 260 million gallons of gasoline annually.

The FY 2014 Loan Programs Office (LPO) Budget Request for ATVM will enable LPO to monitor closed projects and conduct underwriting on new projects.

Advanced Technologies Vehicles Manufacturing Loan Program ($6.0 million)

The FY 2014 Budget Request supports the President's goals to strengthen U.S. leadership in advanced vehicle development and production. The Budget Request also supports American competitiveness in clean energy while responding to the threat of climate change.

- Accelerates the domestic commercial deployment of innovative and advanced clean energy technologies at a scale sufficient to meaningfully contribute to the achievement of our national clean energy objectives—including job creation; reduced dependence on oil; mitigation of greenhouse gas emissions; and enhancement of American competitiveness in the global economy of the 21st century.
- Supports the development of advanced technology vehicles and associated components in the United States.
- Encourages the manufacture of environmentally responsible products through providing growth capital.
- Proactively monitors projects post financial close and manages risks associated with those projects.
- Originates new loans to utilize existing loan authority and appropriated credit subsidy.

Innovative Technology Loan Guarantee Program

	FY 2012 Current	FY 2013 Annualized CR*	FY 2014 Request	FY 2014 vs. FY 2012	
				$	%
Administrative Operations	38,000	---	48,000	+10,000	+26.3%
Loan Guarantee, Offsetting Collections	-38,000	---	-48,000	-10,000	-26.3%
Total, Innovative Technology Loan Guarantee Program	**0**	**0**	**0**	**0**	**N/A**

(discretionary dollars in thousands)

Note: FY 2013 amounts shown reflect the P.L. 112 175 continuing resolution level annualized to a full year. These amounts are shown only at the "congressional control" level and above; below that level a dash (—) is shown.

Innovative Technology Loan Guarantee Program

The Innovative Technology Loan Guarantee Program (LGP), as authorized under Title XVII of the Energy Policy Act of 2005, encourages early commercial use of new or significantly improved technologies in energy projects. Projects supported by DOE loan guarantees must avoid, reduce, or sequester air pollutants or anthropogenic emissions of greenhouse gases; employ new or significantly improved technologies compared to commercial technologies in service in the United States at the time the guarantee is issued; and offer a reasonable prospect of repayment of the principal and interest on the guaranteed obligation. LPO programs support DOE's strategic goal of accelerating transformation of America's energy system and securing U.S. leadership in clean energy technology as well as the President's goals for advancing clean energy. The LGP has closed over $16 billion in loan guarantees for 26 renewable energy projects. The portfolio also includes over $10 billion in conditional commitments that have not yet closed, including loan guarantees for the first new commercial nuclear power plant to be licensed and built in the U.S. in three decades.

The FY 2014 Loan Programs Office (LPO) Budget Request will enable LPO to continue active monitoring of closed projects while increasing efforts to deploy the existing $34 billion in loan authority and $169.6 million in credit subsidy appropriations for clean energy technologies. The FY 2014 Budget Request supports the President's goals to invest in clean energy, innovation, and jobs of the future.

Loan Guarantee Program ($48.0 million)

The FY 2014 Budget Request supports American competitiveness in clean energy while responding to the threat of climate change.

- Accelerates the domestic commercial deployment of innovative and advanced clean energy technologies at a scale sufficient to meaningfully contribute to the achievement of our national clean energy objectives— including job creation; reduced dependence on oil; mitigation of greenhouse gases;
- Supports projects that avoid, reduce, or sequester air pollutants or anthropogenic emissions of greenhouse gases.
- Employs new or significantly improved technologies compared to commercial technologies in service in the United States.
- Proactively monitors projects post financial close and manages risks associated with those projects.
- Originates new loan guarantees to utilize existing loan authority in the nuclear power, front-end nuclear, fossil, and renewable and energy efficiency sectors.

	(discretionary dollars in thousands)				
	FY 2012 Current	FY 2013 Annualized CR	FY 2014 Request	FY 2014 vs. FY 2012	
				$	%
Health, Safety and Security	148,737	149,647	143,616	-5,121	-3.4%
Program Direction	102,000	102,624	108,301	+6,301	+6.2%
Total, Health, Safety and Security	**250,737**	**252,271**	**251,917**	**+1,180**	**+0.5%**

Health, Safety and Security (HSS) demonstrates DOE's unwavering commitment to maintain a safe and secure work environment for all personnel; to ensure that its operations preserve the health, safety, and security of the surrounding communities; and to protect the national security and other entrusted assets. HSS is central to achieving DOE's mission in a safe, secure, environmentally responsible manner by providing sound and consistent policy, technical assistance, training, independent oversight, enforcement, and corporate leadership for HSS program areas.

- **Health and Safety ($73.3 million)**
  Health and Safety provides technical and analytical expertise used to protect and enhance the safety of all DOE workers, the public, and the environment in support of Departmental missions and goals. The subprogram provides for the maintenance of policies and guidance that promote safe, environmentally sustaining work practices throughout DOE to ensure best-in-class performance in the areas of occupational, facility, nuclear, and radiation safety; cultural and natural resources; environment; and quality assurance. Health and Safety provides technical assistance to DOE program and site offices and laboratories through site-specific activities such as nuclear facility safety bases reviews and through corporate-wide services such as accrediting commercial laboratories used by DOE sites for regulatory compliance and employee radiological monitoring programs; reviews of construction projects for high hazard nuclear facilities; and the operation of the Filter Test Facility. It also maintains corporate safety and environmental databases, administers the accident investigation program, supports the radiation emergency accident center, administers the DOE voluntary protection program and assists in the implementation of environmental management systems. Health activities support domestic and international research on exposures of workers and the public to nuclear, radiological, and other materials. It provides health and environmental services to the people of the Marshall Islands; and medical screenings for former DOE and DOE-related vendor employees and supports the Department of Labor (DOL) in implementation of the Energy Employee Occupational Illness Compensation Program Act. The Health and Safety subprogram also provides support for the implementation of the Congressionally-mandated worker safety and health, nuclear safety, and classified information security enforcement programs to ensure contractors' adherence to regulations and to promote ongoing improvement of safety and security.

- **Security ($70.3 million)**
  Security provides technical and analytical expertise support to develop and assist in the implementation of safeguards and security programs that protect national security assets entrusted to DOE; and to implement the U.S. Government nuclear weapons-related technology classification and declassification program. The subprogram provides for the maintenance of policies and guidance related to physical, personnel, and information security and nuclear materials accountability, in order to be responsive to national security needs and evolving threats. Security provides technical assistance to DOE program, site offices and laboratories to implement cost effective security measures tailored to the mission; and DOE-wide assistance via training programs to develop and maintain the proficiency and competency of DOE safety and security personnel. It maintains corporate security-related information management systems to determine the potential for an undue risk to individual sites, DOE, and national security. **Security** also provides for the protection of DOE facilities and information in the National Capital Area and access authorization

investigations for DOE Headquarters personnel. Additionally, **Security** implements the information control program for the U.S. Government to mitigate national security threats by preventing the release of information related to weapons of mass destruction and other information that, if released, has the potential to damage the U.S. energy infrastructure. Support is also provided to review over 400 million pages of historical documents backlogged at the National Archives for potential release as required by Executive Order.

The FY 2014 Budget Request reflects a decreased reliance on contractor support for policy, assistance, and training activities via implementation of efficiencies and increased reliance on the Federal workforce; prioritization of security equipment maintenance and purchases; and elimination of some domestic health research activities in order to increase funding for nuclear safety and enforcement activities and provide for increased former worker medical screening activities. The funding level also reflects an expected decrease in the reinvestigations needed to provide access authorizations as needed; and decrease in FY 2014 Budget Requests for record searches associated with the DOL compensation program. These decreases are partially offset by the transfer of the Telecommunications Security Program (TSP) from the DOE Office of the Chief Information Officer (OCIO) to HSS.

- **Program Direction ($108.3 million)**
Program Direction (PD) provides federal staffing, travel, support services, and other resources required for execution of HSS program activities. PD also provides independent oversight for safeguards and security; cyber security; emergency management, nuclear safety, and environment, safety, and health; providing performance feedback to DOE leadership, program and site offices, and site contractors; and liaison with the Defense Nuclear Facilities Safety Board.

The increase reflects additional resources for nuclear safeguards and security, nuclear safety, and cyber security independent oversight, working capital fund increases, an increase for travel, expected increases to Federal salaries and benefits, and transfer of TSP from the OCIO to HSS. These increases are offset by a reduction of 24 FTEs, elimination of headquarters security mission support services, and a reduction in IT infrastructure costs.

					(discretionary dollars in thousands)	
		FY 2012 Current	FY 2013 Annualized CR	FY 2014 Request	FY 2014 vs. FY 2012	
					$	%
Energy Information Administration		105,000	105,643	117,000	+12,000	+11.4%
Total, Energy Information Administration		**105,000**	**105,643**	**117,000**	**+12,000**	**+11.4%**

The **U.S. Energy Information Administration** (EIA) is the statistical and analytical agency within the U.S. Department of Energy. EIA collects, analyzes, and disseminates independent and impartial energy information to promote sound policymaking, efficient markets, and public understanding of energy and its interaction with the economy and the environment. As the Nation's premier source of energy information, EIA conducts a data collection program covering the full spectrum of energy sources, end uses, and energy flows; generates short- and long-term domestic and international energy projections; and performs timely, informative energy analyses.

The FY 2014 Budget Request maintains its core energy information program and enables EIA to do the following:
- Complete the 2012 Commercial Buildings Energy Consumption Survey, including release of data that provide U.S. benchmarks used to inform investments in new technologies, performance labeling, and energy management practices.
- Launch the 2014 Residential Energy Consumption Survey, which collects information from a nationally representative sample of housing units, including data on energy characteristics of homes, usage patterns, and household demographics.
- Implement National Academy of Sciences recommendations to improve the processes that underlie these complex, multi-year consumption surveys.
- Modernize and streamline data collection processes across its energy supply surveys, including significant upgrades to the systems and processes used to produce the weekly market-moving natural gas and petroleum product inventory reports.
- Enhance the ability to monitor, forecast, and report on international energy developments.
- Upgrade forecasting capabilities by modernizing the National Energy Modeling System.
- Improve and expand customer access to EIA statistics and analyses via its website.

| | (discretionary dollars in thousands) | | | | |
| | FY 2012 Current | FY 2013 Annualized CR | FY 2014 Request | FY 2014 vs. FY 2012 | |
				$	%
Inspector General	42,000	42,257	42,120	+120	+0.3%
Total, Inspector General	**42,000**	**42,257**	**42,120**	**+120**	**+0.3%**

The **Office of the Inspector General** (OIG) promotes the effective, efficient, and economical operation of the programs and operations of DOE, including the National Nuclear Security Administration and the Federal Energy Regulatory Commission, through audits, inspections, investigations and other reviews, while detecting and preventing fraud, waste, abuse, and violations of law.

Statutory requirements direct the IG to conduct an annual evaluation of DOE's information security systems as required by the Federal Information Systems Management Act of 2002. The IG is also charged with reviewing the Department's efforts to track and improve performance, per the Government Performance and Results Modernization Act of 2010. In addition, the IG conducts reviews of the most significant management challenges facing the Department. In addition, the OIG continues to provide oversight activities of the Recovery Act funds.

Since early 2009, a core focus of the OIG has been DOE activities relating to the oversight of the Recovery Act. The OIG is in the process of re-invigorating our efforts on traditional Department programs and operations by identifying actions to enhance the efficiency and effectiveness of agency programs and operations. To this end the OIG will focus its efforts in the following areas:

- **Support Costs.** OIG will assist in identifying potential costs savings in areas such as the estimated $3.5 billion spent each year on National Laboratory support costs.
- **Key Programs and Projects.** OIG will evaluate the efficacy of the Department's management of key programs and projects such as the Environmental Management program, which annually expends approximately $6 billion, and the Hanford Waste Treatment Plant, which annually expends approximately $12.9 billion.
- **NNSA Modernization Efforts.** NNSA is undertaking a massive modernization effort that will involve major projects (e.g., weapons complex transformation) that will benefit from OIG reviews to proactively identify efficient and effective operations.
- **Loan Guarantee Programs.** OIG will hire experts to assist with reviews of the implementation phase of the Loan Guarantee programs. In addition, most agreements extend well into the future and will require reviews to confirm compliance with loan terms and conditions to protect taxpayer interests.
- **Cost Accounting Standards (CAS).** OIG plans to provide increased review of Department contractor's incurred costs and compliance with Cost Accounting Standards. OIG will need contract auditors to perform this work.
- **Contract Review.** OIG will assess the Department's administration of approximately $25 billion in contracts.

	FY 2012 Current	FY 2013 Annualized CR	FY 2014 Request	FY 2014 vs. FY 2012 (discretionary dollars in thousands)	
				$	%
Southeastern Power Administration					
Purchase Power and Wheeling (PPW)	114,870	115,573	93,284	-21,586	-18.8%
Program Direction (PD)	8,428	8,480	7,750	-678	-8.0%
Subtotal, Southeastern Power Administration	*123,298*	*124,053*	*101,034*	*-22,264*	*-18.1%*
Alternative Financing/Offsetting Collections	-123,298	-124,053	-101,034	+22,264	+18.1%
Total, Southeastern Power Administration	*0*	*0*	*0*	*0*	*N/A*
Southwestern Power Administration					
Program Direction (PD)	31,889	32,084	29,939	-1,950	-6.1%
Operation and Maintenance (O&M)	14,346	14,434	13,598	-748	-5.2%
Construction (CN)	10,772	10,838	6,227	-4,545	-42.2%
Purchase Power and Wheeling (PPW)	50,000	50,306	52,000	+2,000	+4.0%
Subtotal, Southwestern Power Administration	*107,007*	*107,662*	*101,764*	*-5,243*	*-4.9%*
Alternative Financing/Offsetting Collection	-95,115	-95,697	-89,872	+5,243	+5.5%
Total, Southwestern Power Administration	*11,892*	*11,965*	*11,892*	*0*	*N/A*
Western Area Power Administration					
Western Area Power Administration Construction, Rehabilitation, Operation, and Maintenance (CROM)					
Operation and Maintenance (O&M)	72,863	73,309	82,843	+9,980	+13.7%
Construction and Rehabilitation (C&R)	110,459	111,125	122,437	+11,978	+10.8%
Purchase Power and Wheeling (PPW)	471,535	474,421	407,109	-64,426	-13.7%
Program Direction (PD)	205,247	206,503	217,709	+12,462	+6.1%
Utah Mitigation and Conservation Fund	3,375	3,396	0	-3,375	-100.0%
Subtotal, Western Area Power Administration (CROM)	*863,479*	*868,754*	*830,098*	*-33,381*	*-3.9%*
Alternative Financing/Offsetting Collection	-767,501	-772,198	-734,168	+33,333	+4.3%
Total, Western Area Power Administration	*95,978*	*96,556*	*95,930*	*-48*	*-0.1%*
Falcon and Amistad Operating and Maintenance Fund	220	221	420	+200	+90.9%
Total, Falcon and Amistad Fund	*220*	*221*	*420*	*+200*	*+90.9%*
Colorado River Basins Power Marketing Fund (CRBPMF)	-23,000	-23,141	-23,000	0	N/A
Total, CRBPMF	*-23,000*	*-23,141*	*-23,000*	*0*	*N/A*
Transmission Infrastructure Program (TIP)					
Operating Expenses	50,098	204,278	30,259	-19,839	-39.6%
Offsetting Collections	-50,098	-204,278	-30,259	+19,839	+39.6%
Total, TIP	*0*	*0*	*0*	*0*	*N/A*
Total, Western Area Power Administration	*73,198*	*73,636*	*73,350*	*+152*	*+0.2%*
Total, Power Marketing Administrations	**85,090**	**85,601**	**85,242**	**152**	**+0.2%**

The four **Power Marketing Administrations** (PMAs) sell electricity primarily generated by federally owned hydropower projects. Preference in the sale of power is given to public entities and electric cooperatives. Revenues from the sale of federal power and transmission services are used to repay all related power costs. The PMAs contribute to the reliability of the nation's electricity supply and electrical grid. The PMAs also facilitate the Department's efforts to transform the Nation's energy system and secure U.S. leadership in clean energy technologies in promoting the development of higher capacity, more expansive U.S. energy infrastructure to support the development and delivery of renewable resources. Specifically, the PMAs are maintaining and modernizing facilities to ensure flexible and reliable operations to accommodate industry change, interconnections and increasing interest in renewable resources; while partnering with industry to expand infrastructure to deliver developing sources of renewable energy.

The FY 2014 Budget Request continues the use of receipts to offset the annual expenses of Western Area Power Administration (Western), Southwestern Power Administration (Southwestern) and Southeastern Power Administration (Southeastern) to allow for better operations and maintenance planning and execution, leading to a more reliable power system. Bonneville Power Administration (Bonneville), unlike the other PMAs, is "self-financed" by the ratepayers of the Pacific Northwest and receives no direct, annual appropriations.

In FY 2014, both Western and Bonneville will continue the development and construction of major transmission projects in their service territories with the borrowing authority they were provided under the Recovery Act. Many of these projects are designed specifically to facilitate the delivery of renewable energy to market.

Southeastern Power Administration ($0.0 million)
Southeastern markets and delivers all available federal hydroelectric power from 22 U.S. Army Corps of Engineers (Corps) multipurpose projects to preference customers in an eleven-state area in the southeastern United States. Southeastern does not own or operate any transmission facilities, and contracts with regional utilities that own electric transmission systems to deliver the federal hydropower to Southeastern's customers. Southeastern's use of receipts and alternative financing offsets its appropriations to result in a net-zero balance for the program.

Southwestern Power Administration ($11.9 million)
Southwestern markets and delivers federal hydroelectric power from 24 Corps multipurpose projects to preference customers in a six-state area and participates with other water resource users in an effort to balance diverse interests with power needs. To deliver power to its customers, Southwestern maintains 1,380 miles of high-voltage transmission lines, 25 substations/switchyards, and 51 microwave and VHF radio sites.

Western Area Power Administration ($73.4 million)
Western markets and transmits federal power to a 1.3-million-square-mile service area in 15 central and western states from 56 federally-owned hydroelectric power plants primarily operated by the Bureau of Reclamation (the Bureau), the Corps, and the International Boundary and Water Commission.

Bonneville Power Administration
Bonneville provides electric power, transmission, and energy services to a 300,000-square-mile service area in eight states in the Pacific Northwest. Bonneville wholesales the power produced at 31 federal projects operated by the Corps and the Bureau and from certain non-federal generating facilities. Bonneville funds the expense portion of its budget, and the power operations and maintenance costs of the Bureau and the Corps in the Federal Columbia River Power System (FCRPS). The capital portion of the budget is funded mostly through borrowing from the U.S. Treasury at market rates for similar projects and with some non-federal financing.

Bonneville receives no direct annual appropriations from Congress. In FY 2014, total requirements of all Bonneville programs include estimated budget obligations of $4.4 billion. This amount includes operating expenses of $3.0 billion, capital investments of $1.2 billion, and $61 million in projects funded in advance; with $132 million in capital transfers. These investments provide electric utility and general plant requirements associated with the FCRPS's transmission services, capital equipment, hydroelectric projects, conservation, and capital investments in environment, fish, and wildlife.

	FY 2012 Current	FY 2013 Annualized CR	FY 2014 Request	FY 2014 vs. FY 2012 (discretionary dollars in thousands)	
				$	%
Federal Energy Regulatory Commission	304,600	306,464	304,600	0	N/A
FERC Revenues	-304,600	-306,464	-304,600	0	N/A
Subtotal, Federal Energy Regulatory Commission	*0*	*0*	*0*	*0*	*N/A*
Excess Fees and Recoveries, FERC					
Fees & Recoveries in Excess of Annual Appropriations	-25,534	-27,479	-26,236	-702	-2.7%
Total, Federal Energy Regulatory Commission	**-25,534**	**-27,479**	**-26,236**	**-702**	**-2.7%**

The **Federal Energy Regulatory Commission (FERC or the Commission)** is an independent agency that regulates the transmission and wholesale sale of electricity in interstate commerce; the transmission and sale of natural gas for resale in interstate commerce; and the transportation of oil by pipeline in interstate commerce. FERC also reviews proposals to build liquefied natural gas (LNG) terminals as well as interstate natural gas pipelines, and licenses and inspects non-federal hydropower projects. The Commission protects the reliability of the Nation's bulk-power system and oversees environmental matters related to natural gas pipeline and non-federal hydro projects. The Commission enforces its regulatory requirements through civil penalties and other means.

FERC's mission is to assist consumers in obtaining reliable, efficient and sustainable energy services at a reasonable cost through appropriate regulatory and market means. FERC seeks to ensure that rates, terms and conditions of service are just, reasonable and not unduly discriminatory or preferential, relying on competitive markets where appropriate. Through its oversight and enforcement authorities, FERC seeks to increase compliance with its rules and regulations and deter market manipulation. FERC's responsibilities also include promoting the development of strong and secure energy infrastructure that operates safely, reliably and efficiently in the public interest.

- **Just and Reasonable Rates, Terms and Conditions ($165.7 million)**
  To ensure just and reasonable rates, terms and conditions of service, the Commission will rely on competition and appropriate regulatory policies. Competition will benefit energy consumers by encouraging new entry among supply-side and demand-side resources, spurring innovation and deployment of new technologies, improving operating performance and exerting downward pressure on costs. The Commission will pursue policy reforms to ensure that all types of resources operate on a level playing field in jurisdictional markets. These reforms will specifically address the emergence of demand resources and renewable resources, barriers to participation by such resources in wholesale electric markets and best practices in organized markets to help achieve the potential benefits associated with demand response.

  The Commission seeks to ensure that its market and other regulatory rules are clear, enforceable, and fully understood by the regulated entities. While the obligation to comply with those rules lies with the regulated entity itself, the Commission is actively pursuing a strategy to promote rigorous internal compliance programs. The Commission also takes proactive steps to reduce the probability that violations will occur, including conducting compliance audits and performing investigations. FERC will continue to place additional emphasis on activities that disrupt or impair the functioning of competitive energy markets. Where appropriate, FERC will exercise its civil penalty authority of up to $1 million per day for the duration of the violation.

- **Energy Infrastructure ($138.9 million)**
  The Commission has an important role in the development of efficient, safe, reliable and secure energy infrastructure. The Commission will implement rate treatment policies that support investments in smart grid

technologies where appropriate. FERC will continue to support an open and transparent electric transmission planning process. Such coordination between transmission providers will support the development of an efficient transmission system and enhance competition in wholesale electric markets.

The Commission's infrastructure siting authority rests in licensing non-federal hydropower projects, certificating interstate natural gas pipelines and storage projects, authorizing LNG facilities and, in certain circumstances, permitting electric transmission lines. Post-authorization, the Commission relies heavily on physical inspections of hydropower and LNG facilities to ensure safety.

Maintaining the reliability of the Nation's electric transmission grid is a critical responsibility of the Commission. FERC will oversee the development and enforcement of mandatory electric reliability standards and critical infrastructure protection standards. In addition, the Commission will provide leadership, expertise and assistance to identify, communicate and seek comprehensive solutions to potential risks to Commission-jurisdictional facilities from cyber attacks and certain physical threats.